Beyond Five Minutes

Lessons From a Wounded Warrior's Life Outdoors

Jack Zimmerman

Beyond Five Minutes

Lessons From A Wounded Warrior's Life Outdoors

Jack Zimmerman

Published by Austin Brothers Publishing, Fort Worth, Texas

www.abpbooks.com

Scanning, uploading, and distribution of this book without permission by the publisher is theft of the author's intellectual property. To obtain permission to use material from the book (other than for review purposes) contact books.by.abp@gmail.com.

ISBN: 979-8-9921929-0-2

Printed in the United States of America

2024 -- First Edition

Copyright © 2024 by Jack Zimmerman

All rights reserved.

No part of this book may be reproduced in any form or by any electronic or mechanical means, including information storage and retrieval systems, without written permission from the author, except for the use of brief quotations in a book review.

Dedication

This book is dedicated to every outdoorsman and woman who came before me, paving the way for the generations behind me. To the guys who pulled me off the battlefield that day and the incredible people who put me back together, without you, none of this would be possible.

To those who got me back into the woods and continue to help me chase my outdoor dreams, your support means more than words can express.

But most of all, to my boys. I hope they come to share the same deep love for the outdoors and the wild as I do.

To all who have contributed to conservation efforts, whether through actions big or small, thank you for ensuring the land, the wildlife, and the traditions we love will continue to thrive for future generations.

Finally, to my best friend, CPL Brett Land, who was killed in Afghanistan. I dedicate everything I do in this life to him. His spirit lives on in everything I pursue, and his memory will always be with me.

— Jack Zimmerman

Author's Note

As you read this book, I invite you to reflect on the true meaning of hunting. It's not about taking down monsters or pile pictures.

Hunting, at its core, is about the people we spend time with in the pursuit of the game we love.

It's about the bonds formed around campfires, the shared stories that echo through the woods, and the respect we develop for the land and the creatures that inhabit it.

We all evolve as hunters. Whether you're just beginning your journey or have spent a lifetime in the wild, this evolution is constant.

As you open this book, I ask you to consider the sportsman you are now, the values you hold,

Author's Note

the reasons you step into the outdoors, and the legacy you wish to leave behind.

But this is more than just a personal journey. It's about ensuring we always have a place in the outdoors, not just for ourselves but for future generations.

It's about preserving the traditions and the wild places that we hold dear.

When you turn the final page, I hope you'll reflect on the sportsman you want to become.

Let this book be a guide, a companion on your journey, as you continue to grow in your respect for the hunt, the land, and the people who share this passion with you.

–Jack Zimmerman

Contents

Foreword	ix
Introduction	xiii
1. Not Done Yet	1
2. The Making of a Hunter	9
3. Adaptability	23
4. Making Changes	31
5. Unbreakable	43
6. Man's Best Friend	55
7. Leaning on Others	63
8. Camaraderie	71
9. Wetting a Line	81
10. The Next Generation	89
11. Gratitude, Awe, and Resilience	105
12. A New Perspective	117
13. Looking Toward the Future	125

Foreword

Jack and I first crossed paths over 10 years ago on a hunt in South Texas, where wounded veterans were given an opportunity to get back outdoors, fellowship with others who had been through similar experiences, and use their rifles again. For me, it was one of those moments that stick with you for the rest of your life—one of those moments when you know you've met someone whose story will stay with you long after the hunting trip ends.

Over the course of several nights sitting beside campfires and several days of hunting, Jack shared his journey with me about his time of service in the military. He shared not only the things he loved about serving our great country but also the sacrifices he made—mentally and physically. At the time, I was so taken aback by the fact that a man who had been blown up, lost the ability to walk for the rest of his life, and seen so much horror could talk about all of it as if it were just another day at work—just another thing he was going to overcome no matter what. That alone is a testament to who Jack is. He's not just a soldier; he's an inspiring person.

Years after our encounter in South Texas, we met up again when I played a show in his hometown, and since then, we've crossed paths many times. I've had the privilege of seeing Jack at my concerts over the years, and to this day, it's still an honor every time I get to reconnect with him. For me, each reconnection is a reminder of the sacrifices made every day by our great American heroes so the rest of us can live free in the greatest country in the world.

What struck me most about Jack back then—and still moves me to this very day—wasn't just his resilience; it was his positivity and faith through all the adversity he faced during his time of service. I have to admit that I'm somewhat jealous of, yet full of admiration for, the way he continues to live with purpose and use his true story to inspire others. That's what this book, Beyond Five Minutes, is all about.

Jack Zimmerman shows us that no matter how deep the hole, how dark the night, or how far we've fallen, we have the ability to rise again.

And again...

And again...

One thing that's always been important to me is honoring those who serve—namely, our first responders, police, and military. At every one of my concerts, I take the time to pay tribute to them and will continue to do so for the rest of my career. People like Jack Zimmerman remind me why that moment during each show matters. The sacrifices they've made, the baggage and hurt they carry for our freedom—that is what MATTERS. These people are what keep the heart of this country beating strong! Jack's story is one I'm so proud to know and even prouder to share with all of you reading this.

As you read Beyond Five Minutes, you'll see why Jack's journey is more than just one of survival. It's a story of triumph. It's a story of living with purpose. And, even more importantly, it's a story of never letting life's toughest moments define who you are. Jack Zimmerman is a symbol of the unbreakable American spirit, and I'm honored to call him a friend.

— *Cody Johnson, award-winning country artist*

Introduction

Five minutes.

It doesn't seem like a long time, but it might be, depending on the circumstances. If you're a student cramming for a final exam, five minutes isn't long. If you're a kid waiting for your dad to come outside and play catch, it might seem like an eternity.

If you're rapidly losing blood and fighting for consciousness, five minutes seemed like an impossible amount of time. Lying in the back of a truck after getting off a MEDEVAC chopper, the surgeon looked at me and told me if I could stay awake for five more minutes, he promised me I would live. It was the most pivotal moment that day, perhaps even my entire life. Five minutes seemed like an unbearable amount of time.

Platoon

It was March 9, 2011. The air was cool as the sun came up. My day started in Guard Tower 3, looking out over our COP (company outpost) in Afghanistan. The COP sat near a man-made mountain that was visible from miles around. It was obviously chosen for its strategic location. There wasn't a huge number of troops in the COP, maybe two platoons consisting of fewer than 100 guys. Our primary task was to patrol the area, find the enemy, push the Taliban out of the area, and make the area safe. Our days were typically long, so when I came down from the guard tower after being relieved, I knew there was still much to do before the day was over.

Introduction

I carried my SAW (squad automatic weapon) and other gear, including night vision equipment, and returned to my bed. I always carried about 1,200 rounds with me, along with all the other stuff needed by a soldier. The area is super sandy, looking like what I envision as moon dust, and it's hard to keep from tracking it inside the tent. There are always a few guys sitting at the front door, smoking, joking, or eating. I walked past them, made a few jokes and some small talk before going to my bunk to drop off my stuff.

My bunkmate was asleep in the top bunk. It was always dark in the tent as someone was always sleeping because of the different schedules. The front of the tent was for platoon leaders and others of higher rank. That was also the area where plans were made, and assignments distributed each day. A giant whiteboard contained a "to-do" list of who was doing what. I was assigned to go on patrol for the day.

Two teams were designated to go out together, and it noted that Z-man, my nickname, was assigned to carry the litter, which consisted of a three-foot cylinder that contained the fold-out stretcher used for carrying the wounded. I took notes in my notebook of the assignment and returned to my bunk for a quick nap.

About a half-hour later, someone came by and hit me, saying, "Hey, we're going to a briefing for the patrol."

Outside, we noticed everyone going on patrol was reviewing assignments and a map of the area. We would be northeast of Ahmad Khan; we called it "AK" for short. It was in the Arghandab River Valley.

Weeks earlier, when we first arrived at this place, all the stuff was still packed in the Conex box used for delivery, so nothing was set up. Our first task was to deploy the tents and get everything inflated and up and running. I was an electrician before joining the Army, so my skills came in handy, which meant I was heavily involved in setting up the entire COP. We were now living at Ahmad Khan, a place surrounded by opium and marijuana fields as far as you could see.

One of the crazy things about our location is that it was near the largest Taliban graveyard. We would go on patrol and kill a Taliban. Within a few days, we could observe the funeral just a quarter of a mile away in the cemetery for those we killed.

Our patrol set out to scout a teardrop-shaped area consisting of several villages. Our COP was at the base of the teardrop, so we headed north. We came to a large spread of villages but understand,

Introduction

when I use the term "village," I'm describing a maze of buildings where people live. They are all connected, but it doesn't make any sense. Walls are everywhere, six or eight feet high. They are not stand-alone houses like you would find in a U.S. community.

The walls were constructed with bricks. Each brick was hand-made from mud, straw, and cow chips. They were stacked and hardened. Seperate buildings, called grape huts, were placed at intervals in the wall, and these were used to hang grapevines. These huts had a roof to keep the rain from the grapes. The walls were so compacted and solid that it was impossible to tell the wall had been shot up after a gunfight. They provided great protection for the Taliban as they used them for cover, firing their weapons through openings.

We pushed our way north and east and came to a large spread of villages. Taliban were active in this area, so confrontation with enemy forces was expected whenever we went on patrol. Upon arriving in Afghanistan, survival depends on emotionally adapting to these circumstances. You learn to live with the knowledge that something devastating can happen at any moment, but you still must function normally and carry on daily routines. This particular patrol fit that pattern.

Introduction

We knew something was going on because we saw a large group of guys going in and out of the area surrounding the village. We assumed they had a cache of weapons and ammo, so our job was to find and destroy the cache. We anticipated a fight as we prepared to head out on patrol.

All of us had our gear near the ECP (Entrance Control Point) as we got in formation and set out on the mission. My team was on point, Sergeant Hurley in the front and I was on the right flank. Picture this like a flock of geese. Two riflemen were with us that day on the other flank and behind all of us was the platoon leader. Our First Sergeant was with us, and the gun team was behind, along with the interpreters as well as another entire team.

It was late in the morning when we pushed out, encountering villages where we had been several times before. We had become friends with one of the elders, so we stopped and visited for a few minutes. I remembered one guy because his son was always with him, but he was not around this day. Part of the job was to get to know the locals; they could be friends or enemies; it was hard to tell. As the Saw Gunner, I stayed on the perimeter, interacting with the locals to a small extent. It was an incredibly hostile area, and even talking to friendly locals required being alert.

We tried to keep everyone at a distance because of the fear of suicide bombers or vehicle-borne IEDs (Improvised Explosive Devices) like a motorcycle or car. We continued north, taking our time. It was spring, so there wasn't any vegetation, which meant no cover or concealment anywhere. That meant we could see any potential trap. The rainy season had recently ended, so we were walking across bare plowed fields.

We continued working our way toward the top of the village. There was a large berm on the north end, and I remember running up to the top and looking down into the town. I immediately saw two guys running. I hollered to Sergeant Hurley, "Hey, we got two guys running to town."

From my experience, I knew those guys were up to no good and were likely the guys we were looking for. As soon as I called out, I looked down and realized I was standing on top of an IED. Spotting an IED was not unusual. Often, they were nothing more than an old shell casing or dirty plastic jug filled with fuel, topped with nails and screws. When exploded, the nails and screws were propelled, seeking flesh.

It was obvious; the two guys were putting in

IEDs before I saw them running. I scurried down the berm to watch the building the guys entered. The Sergeant put a charge on the IED to blow it up as I kept watching the buildings. The gun team was ninety degrees to my right and set up on a wall that looked toward the building; we were in a horseshoe shape around the building.

As soon as Sergeant Hurley detonated the IED, they began shooting at us, apparently thinking we were shooting at them. The gunfight was on. I had one guy pinned in the doorway as the gun team was throwing rounds into the buildings. As we were fighting, suddenly I realized that somebody got around us. We were taking rounds from the side, and a guy worked his way around through the ditch.

I remember returning fire on him and staying engaged back and forth while the others continued firing into the building. At that moment, the Kiowa helicopters arrived, throwing Hellfires into the buildings, and the gunfire wrapped up quickly. When it was over, we took a few minutes for a smoke and to regroup before heading back to the COP. The plan was to resupply ammo and water and come back to find the cache.

Leaving, we were in reverse order movement,

Introduction

so I was now in the back of the formation on the left flank, still as the SAW Gunner. We followed the ditch out of the village, walking north. The enemy was close so we jumped across the ditch. Since I was in the back, I was the last to cross. I was walking in my buddy's footsteps in front of me, step by step. The field was open as far as you could see, and it was huge.

We were skirting the village and knew the enemy was close. Weeks earlier, we located IED making material, so we knew it was a hotspot.

The Sergeant said, "Hey Jackie boy, they're going to hit us again."

"Where do you think they're gonna hit us from," I replied.

He said, "I don't know, Jackie boy."

We had an interpreter with us listening in on the radios and he could hear the chatter. He could hear that we were going to get attacked again so he told the Lieutenant.

I didn't have time to laugh or respond. I remember feeling like I just took off, blasted like a rocket. It felt like a really bad, horrible dream, feeling you're never going to wake up, the kind when you wake up feeling clammy with sweaty palms. Only this time, I couldn't wake up. It felt like I was falling forever. At the same time, I had the sensation of 10,000 miniature fingers running up my back, like a flashy heat of 10,000 skin pricks. I remember tumbling and tumbling and tumbling like it was never going to end.

I remember thinking to myself and trying to figure out what the hell was going on. I didn't know if I was hit by Afghan army soldiers, an RPG, or what. I didn't know. I do remember landing on my left black flank, and my shoulder or neck hit the ground. It recalled an experience as a kid, falling on a playground from high up and landing on my back.

It was totally silent because I couldn't hear anything. I looked around to figure out what was going on, but I was disoriented. As I surveyed things, I noticed my left arm. My shirt's entire sleeve was blown off, and the backside of my arm was completely gone. That's when I knew I needed a tourniquet. I knew I had to tie off my left arm to stop the bleeding.

It was the only injury I noticed at the time, so I tried to get my first-aid kit. It was on my left side toward my back. I always carried it on that side in case I was ever shot. I could continue to shoot with my right hand and perform first aid with my left. However, my left shoulder popped when I landed, and I couldn't reach my arm back

Introduction

far enough to retrieve anything from the first-aid kit.

By this time, a lot of blood had run out of my arm, and I knew a tourniquet was vital. I knew there was one in my night vision pouch in my right-side gear. I grabbed that pouch, and it was at that moment that I noticed the smallest piece of skin, three-quarters of the way up my forearm was the only thing keeping my arm from falling off. I picked up my arm, and every time my heartbeat, I could see blood gush from the back of my arm. At that point, it dawned on me that I was in trouble.

Tracer rounds filled the air above my head as my hearing gradually returned. Faint sounds of gunfire were the first thing I heard, but I didn't have my SAW. With each passing second, it became more and more obvious I was in a really bad situation. It took some time for me to realize I had stepped on an IED.

At this point, I had no idea my legs were hurt. I was sitting in a crater, and my guts hurt so bad, like I had been smacked in the balls with a baseball bat. Reeling from the pain, I curled up, trying to find some comfort.

Suddenly, my buddy Daniels slid in on top of me and began working on me. He opened both of our first-aid kits and put a tourniquet on both my arms. I tried to stay low since we were in a crater, engaged with the enemy in a firefight. If I had seen all my injuries the way he did, I might have been tempted to give up, but he kept repeating, "You're gonna be all right."

Still unable to feel everything, I responded, "Hey man, you got to get off me, you know, you're pinching my boys."

It felt like he was kneeling on my nuts as he worked on me. The next thing I knew, Doc slid into the hole and immediately went to work. Doc and I were close friends, and he was frantic as he threw his bag down. Doc was from Wisconsin, and since I came from Minnesota, we felt like neighbors, and he was like my "number two."

When he got my gear off, I tried to sit up, thinking I would move to cover. At that point, I realized my right leg had been completely torn off. Within a matter of seconds, I saw that my left leg was also in bad shape. It looked like one of those Halloween decorations where all you see is the bones with my boot dangling at the end. My first thought was about the possibility of hopping on one leg to get to a better spot. I could see how many guys were occupied with me and became frightened about the situation.

It's impossible to describe what was going

through my mind. There was a measure of fear of being hit again since we were in the middle of a live firefight, bullets whizzing around. The pain from my catastrophic wounds was beginning to set in, and as my hearing returned, the noise was deafening. All of that was clouded by my desire to avoid being a burden on my team. I didn't want more guys taken away from the fight because of my injuries.

It was obvious that I had to let someone else take over. They talked to me about what to do, even bringing up trivial subjects to get my mind off the situation. Daniels and I planned to get a house together when we got home, and he brought that up. He reminded me I would bring my girlfriend down and other stuff we had anticipated as if it were still going to happen.

I was getting tired, so, so tired. Everyone was talking and working hard on me. My right leg was torn off almost to the groin, and Doc struggled to find the artery to tie it off. He was finally able to grab it, and it hurt so bad. I was being overtaken by exhaustion, and it was a struggle to remain conscious. I remember looking up at the sun beaming into my eyes, thinking this is the place where I'm going to die.

The guys kept talking to me, trying to keep me

going. I insisted that I couldn't talk anymore; I didn't have the energy. The thirst was almost unbearable; I was ready to kill someone for a drink. Doc gave me some water on a piece of gauze that he stuck in the corner of my mouth. It was surprisingly satisfying. Thinking I was at the end of my life, that tiny bit of moisture on my lips felt good.

My method for staying alive was to keep telling myself, "Left, right, left, right," as I rolled my head back and forth. It was a way to focus on something I could do that required conscious effort. However, that soon stopped working, and I told the guys, "I think this is it." Something happened at that moment—I could feel myself. It was almost euphoric, incredibly peaceful. The pain was gone; it was surreal. I think it was shock more than anything, but I was at peace with living or dying at that point. I was able to turn my power to something greater than myself, if that makes sense.

When you're lying there and all this chaos is going around you, it gets very quiet—eerily quiet. Everything just kind of starts fading out, and it takes a minute for everything to come into focus.

Memories flashed before my eyes, vivid as the day they happened. Playing baseball with my buddies as a kid, riding bikes around my little

Introduction

Minnesota hometown. The laughter and freedom of driving around with friends in high school. Sitting peacefully for hours in a deer stand I had built. The thrill when a buck finally passed into view. Harvesting that first buck.

Seeing my life flash before my eyes—and wanting to make more of those memories—gave me the strength to draw in one more breath and face the chaos that was coming.

My right leg was completely gone; my left leg was barely there. I was waiting on the battlefield, rapidly bleeding out, with not much to hang on to. I was conscious enough to hear the "woof, woof, woof" of chopper blades approaching. I refused to be that guy who dies the moment the helicopter arrives. *These guys came to save my life,* I thought. *I can't give up. They are risking their own lives to save mine.*

I was critically low on blood, and the guys flipped me up. Doc was jabbing the needle into my neck, trying to find a vein. Finally, he said, "Alright, we just got to go. We've got to get him on the chopper."

I remember being rolled over onto my left side and then rolled back onto the litter. Even though I had been assigned to carry the litter, I had carried something for Daniels on patrol a few days earlier, so he carried the litter for me that day. Otherwise, the litter would have been thrashed, and I might not have made it off the battlefield. They picked me up, and I had the feeling it was all over for me. I could see my left foot lying on my chest as they sprinted with me on the litter, pain shooting through me with every bounce. As they slid me through the door, it was the absolute worst feeling I had the entire day. I looked up and saw Sergeant Hurley already seated in the back of the chopper, and I didn't know if he was alive or dead. He was hunched over as the flight medic and Doc were talking.

I heard the flight medic say, "I don't give a shit; we got to go."

Doc was trying to tell him what he had done, but the medic didn't care. We were still in the middle of a gunfight, and he wanted to get off the ground. I learned later that when the IED under me blew up, a big chunk of steel flew up and bounced off Sergeant Hurley's shoulder, hit him in the head, and knocked him goofy.

With an incredible concussion, he looked at me and said, "Hey, man, you're in tough shape." I didn't sense a lot of confidence in his voice, and I felt like the end was coming.

During our flight to Kandahar, the flight medic

worked frantically, punching a huge needle into my chest. The pain shocked me alert again. I watched him squeeze the IV bag, pushing life back into me.

As we landed at the Kandahar Airfield, I noticed something was different. Usually, when we landed at the forward operating base, everything was fast—quick landings, rapid exits. But this time, I heard the rotors slowly winding down. It was a strange, unfamiliar sound inside a helicopter.

As those rotors slowed, it felt like a transition. The chaos of the battlefield was fading, giving me a moment to collect my thoughts and comprehend what had just happened. It was a brief respite, a chance to regroup and reset my mindset for the next challenge ahead.

The chopper door opened, and suddenly the real chaos began. They pulled me out and loaded me into the back of a truck with an ambulance-style box. An anesthesiologist was on my left, and a surgeon was on my right.

The surgeon looked me in the eye and said, "If you can stay awake for five more minutes, I promise you your life."

On the cusp between life and death, the surgeon's words stuck with me and gave me something to hold onto. They became my mission, my focus. Just five more minutes. I could do that. I *had* to do that. And with every ounce of will I had left, I fought to keep my eyes open, determined to live.

The surgeon had believed I could make it, and that had made all the difference. My battle was far from over, but I had a deeper well of strength to draw from than I ever realized.

It's funny how a few words from a stranger can change everything. I didn't know his name, his story, anything about him. But in that moment, he became my lifeline. He saw something in me, a spark of determination, a will to live that perhaps even I hadn't fully recognized in myself. And he made a promise, a vow that if I held up my end of the bargain, if I could just hang on a little longer, he would do everything in his power to save me.

I held on to that promise like it was the only thing tethering me to this world. In a way, it was. The pain was excruciating, the temptation to let go, to slip away into that beckoning darkness, was overwhelming. But every time I felt myself fading, I would hear his words again, see his face, and it would jolt me back. Just five more minutes. I could do that. I *had* to do that.

Those five minutes felt like an eternity, and

although they're just a tiny fraction of my life so far, they changed what it would become.

His promise was truly the pivotal moment of the day. In the most chaotic moments of my life, that one thing was simple: I needed to hang on for five more minutes.

> *It will forever be my greatest honor to have served in the company of men like Jack Zimmerman. Jack and I became fast friends through a shared experience of us both growing up in the Midwest with similar hobbies and interests such as hunting, fishing, and sports. Jack was a welcome addition to the platoon, coming into pre-deployment training and the ramp-up of team-building prior to heading into Kandahar province.*
>
> *He brought a lighthearted attitude when switched off and a laser focus when switched on that was emulated by Jack's peers. This quickly made Jack a "glue" member of Second Platoon.*
>
> *As the platoon medic, I made it my goal to provide a sense of confidence in everyone to fight without fear of injury because "Doc will come fix you up." I took*

Introduction

this goal seriously and was responsible for our platoon's individual First Aid training from top to bottom.

The classes we'd do were not of the 'downtime' or 'joke and smoke' variety. We had a special group of soldiers... 50% professional and 50% badass at all times. After months of fighting, we were like a well-oiled machine built on hard work. Iron very much sharpened iron among the soldiers of Second Platoon and Charlie Company as a whole.

"ICOM chatter says we're going to get hit again!" yelled Sergeant Johnson, just as the shockwave of sound and plume of smoke rolled over the hill. My heart sank as I ran toward the blast. *I need to go to work*, I thought to myself as I sprinted through our strung-out file that was a mixed formation in the middle of a reversal of movement.

I came over the hill to find Jack torn up badly, with additional platoon members giving and receiving First Aid while actively fighting the fight of incoming small arms fire directly to my left. I ran through half of my tracer magazine on a *window where I saw flashes of movement, while moving toward and sliding into the small crater Jack had ended up in.*

Mitch (Daniels) and I worked in unison; he controlled bleeding to Jack's upper extremities with CATs (tourniquets) while trying to keep Jack calm, and I worked through managing the injuries to Jack's lower half. I drove the edge of my knee deep into Jack's left groin as I worked to apply both a ratchet strap and SOF-T type tourniquet to what remained of Jack's right leg.

Transferring to his left leg, I applied two CATs, pressing down the torn musculature of his femur in an effort to be as high above the wounds sustained as possible in hopes that his femoral artery had not separated and retracted above the leg.

With major hemorrhagic bleeding under control, I moved to packing and bandaging puncture wounds with wet gauze and occlusive dressings to Jack's midsection. Jack was asking for water (which I didn't want to give him because of the injuries to his abdomen) so I stuck a wad of wet gauze to the side of Jack's cheek to give him some relief. Marty (Martinez) and I completed the 9-Line at this point, and we were given a six-minute time to wheels down.

At this point, I was looking to get Jack some fluids to keep him out of hemorrhagic shock and dug deep into my bag for my Fast-1 IO (intra-osseous) kit, as all extremity veins (for IV access) had now been stopped with tourniquets. Upon inspection, I found the spring mechanism necessary to release a needle through Jack's sternum was damaged and unusable. I transitioned to IV access via the External Jugular vein and found that his carotid pulse was becoming weak and thready with his veins non-palpable. I made two attempts to fish each side of his neck for a flash of vein, and failed in both sides.

"Two minutes!" Marty called, and we moved quickly to load Jack onto the SKED Litter and move him to the hasty LZ, a short 50-meter distance away. We could see the medical chopper heading in toward our smoke as we crossed the terrain toward a flat piece of farm field to load.

Wheels down. I help load Jack and

grab the flight medic to give him a rundown of injuries and treatments, hollering over the whir of the rotors... "All four extremities, arterial bleeding controlled! Entries with no exit to lower left and lower right quadrants! No fluid resuscitation or IV access yet. He needs a bag of Hextend, or he's going to shock out!"

The flight medic gave me a nod, and I moved back quickly, listening to the increasing hum of the rotors as the Blackhawk Helicopter banked off of the LZ to the North. As the bird hit the horizon line, I prayed, "Lord, please do not take my friend today. Give him strength to endure."

The moments of Jack's alive day live rent-free in my mind now and forever.

— Lucas "Doc" Nehring

Chapter 1

Not Done Yet

In the operating room, the anesthesiologist told me to count backward from 10, but that wasn't what I did. I knew those seconds could be my last, and I wasn't going to let my last memory on earth be "...one."

Instead, I focused on what mattered—those same memories that had revisited me on the battlefield.

The moments of joy and exhilaration I'd experienced outdoors.

The moments that had made my life worth saving.

I wanted to wake up and make more of them.

Beeping. Pumps hissing. Muffled voices that sounded like Snoopy. I felt like I was deep underwater, rising slowly to the surface. Flashes of memory penetrated the darkness behind my eyelids. The blast. The crater. The MEDEVAC. Was I still alive?

"Jack, say something so we know you can hear us," my dad said. As my vision came into focus, I saw my family surrounding my bed, their faces etched with worry and relief.

"What do I have to do to get the hell out of here?" I croaked, my throat raw and dry. There were tears and laughter. I was alive. I'd made it. But there was a long road still ahead.

I was covered in bandages from top to bottom, and the pain was a dull ache everywhere. I couldn't pinpoint exactly where it hurt most, and I 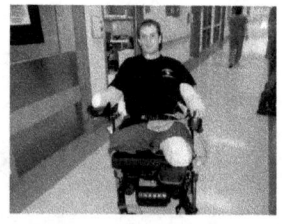 couldn't move. Looking down, I saw tape, monitors, and sensors all over. I could hear the pumps going off—those were my wound vacuum devices, sucking fluid from my injuries. It looked like my arms were intact, but they were wrapped in so many bandages that I couldn't see how extensive the damage was.

As the fog started to lift in those first couple of days, I began to understand the gravity of my situation. My right leg was gone. My left leg had been amputated at the knee. Both my arms were in really bad shape. I kept thinking I needed to call my buddies and tell them I was alive, but I couldn't have even held a phone then—my hands were shredded.

I was broken, but I was alive. I knew my life would never be the same. But a fire was already burning inside me—a determination to not just survive, but to thrive. My journey of recovery and rediscovery was just beginning.

In the days and weeks that followed, I thought back to the memories that had come to me out there in the dirt and the words of the surgeon.

More than anything, I wanted to be worth saving—I wanted the efforts of the men who had saved me to go toward letting me live a life of purpose. I dreamed of getting back out into the woods, of feeling the sun and wind on my face again, of the quiet anticipation of the hunt. It seemed impossible, given my injuries. But I held onto that dream like a lifeline. I pictured myself drawing a bow, drawing down on a deer, and tasting the freedom of the outdoors again. And I knew I would do whatever it took to make that vision a reality.

The first sip of water after what felt like an eternity of thirst. The promise of life. The words of encouragement from a stranger. The call of the wild. These were the things that had saved me and would continue to save me. Lying there in that hospital bed, I knew my fight was just beginning. No matter what it took, no matter how long, I would keep living in the truest sense of the word. I was not done yet. Not by a long shot.

Having someone believe in me, even in my darkest moment, was the beginning of that path toward my new life. The surgeon's belief had been a powerful force, and it filled me with a resolve that went beyond stubbornness or the instinct to survive. It was a sense that I mattered. If someone I had never met before could have that much faith in me and see that much value in my life, then I owed it to him, to the guys who dragged me off the battlefield, to myself, and to everyone who loved me to keep going.

I realized that sometimes, all it takes is one person, one moment of connection, to change the course of a life. That lesson stayed with me. Through the grueling months of surgeries, physical therapy, and the emotional rollercoaster of adapting to my new reality and redefining my place in the world, I held onto that core of belief: that I could overcome anything as long as I had faith in myself and others had faith in me.

As I began to recover and connect with other warriors, I discovered a whole community of people who believed in me and saw in me the same strength and resilience that the surgeon had seen that day. They lifted me up, pushed me forward, and reminded me on the days when I stumbled or fell that I was not alone—and that I was stronger than I knew.

My "tour of duty" in the hospital lasted eight weeks, and during that time I underwent more than 20 surgeries. Two of the weeks were in the Intensive Care Unit (ICU). I was fortunate. Spending so much time on the battlefield, I'd watched many Taliban soldiers get injured, and they were often stuffed into the back of a car and dragged off to whatever they used as a field hospital. I'd had a chopper with experienced medics fly me out of danger and take me to some of the finest medical facilities in the world. State-of-the-art machines and every other necessary device were available. Even infections that would have been deadly to many soldiers were treatable. I received the kind of care that promised a future.

Jack (right) with Cpl. Brett Land

Just coming back to the States, where so many things were already in place, was huge for me. A few months earlier, I had watched my best friend, Cpl. Brett Land, get killed by the very same thing I experienced. He wasn't able to leave the battlefield alive, not able to meet his daughter. My perspective from the beginning was to thank God that I was still alive. Now, it was up to me to decide what to do with the life I had almost lost.

> *I was fortunate enough to work with Jack as his physical therapist at the Center for the Intrepid. We would spend many hours together, five days a week, for months, finding ways for Jack to gain strength, learn to move his new body, and make attainable goals for his future. It is easy to learn quite a bit about a person when you spend that much time together.*
>
> *Rehabilitation after an injury like his is, in one simple word, hard.*
>
> *Jack tackled these hard tasks with a sense of humor and a smile. He never quit, and he always did what was asked of him, even when he disagreed with the plan. Case in point, it was a requirement for patients to participate in the CFI mini-triathlon as part of their rehabilitation. Jack wasn't happy with the requirement, but he trained with the group and put in the work. To be sure we all knew his opinion of the event, he smiled proudly as he rolled to the starting line with a shirt that said, "Running Sucks" and jokingly complained loudly to all that would listen at the finish line.*
>
> *From the first day we met, Jack focused*

on the future, made functional goals for a long and successful life, and was grateful for the life he almost lost. I am thankful that Jack taught me to laugh through the pain and to keep moving forward. We could all learn a lot about resilience from Jack.

— *Alicia White Vanlandingham*

Chapter 2

The Making of a Hunter

Growing up in a little town in southern Minnesota, the outdoors was my whole world. When I wasn't in school or working, you could find me exploring the woods and fields around Cleveland, imagining the day I'd be old enough to join all the other sportsmen in my area out in the field. I'd spend hours in my dad's shop, staring up at the massive deer antlers hanging on the wall, dreaming of the adventures and stories behind each one.

Even before I was old enough to hunt myself, I was obsessed with anything related to the outdoors. Whenever I encountered someone I knew hunted, I grilled them about hunting, soaking up every detail of their stories. I'd ride my bike around town, checking out what was hanging up around town, brought home by hunters. I was hungry for any scrap of information that would help me prepare for my own future hunts.

When I was finally old enough to tag along on a real hunt, I could hardly contain my excitement. I remember the day like it was yesterday—a local farmer, Paul Dauk, promised to take me out deer hunting that evening. I was ready hours early, bundled up in my warmest gear, a bottle of water clutched in my gloved hand as I waited impatiently in the driveway. When Paul finally pulled up, fifteen minutes late, it felt like an eternity had passed. But even that small delay couldn't dampen my enthusiasm. I was going hunting!

We made our way out to one of Paul's favorite spots, settling onto a fallen log beside a drainage ditch. As the sun sank below the horizon and the woods deepened into shadow, every rustle and snap set my nerves jangling. At one point, I was sure I could hear deer moving through the woods —only to see a turkey strutting into view a moment later. Though we never saw a single deer that night, it hardly mattered. I was hooked. The patience, the alertness, the tingling sense of possibility—I knew I had found my calling.

That first taste of hunting only fueled my

passion. I took every opportunity to tag along with my buddies' dads and their friends—anyone who would allow me to join them—even if it was just carrying a BB gun on a pheasant hunt. There was something about being out there with those men, feeling the weight of responsibility and camaraderie, that made me feel ten feet tall. I was part of the team, part of something bigger than myself. And I knew I would do whatever it took to prove that I belonged and earn my place among those seasoned hunters.

The year I was finally old enough to take my firearms safety course was a major milestone. I approached it with a seriousness and intensity that surprised even my instructors. No one had ever accused me of being a scholar—school was just something I had to get through—but all of a sudden, I was soaking in the information like a sponge. For me, it wasn't just a rite of passage—it was a sacred responsibility. When I passed the course and got that certification card, I felt like I had finally taken my first step toward earning my place in the hunting community.

That first deer season, the anticipation was almost unbearable. I must have checked and rechecked my gear a thousand times. The night before opening day, I barely slept a wink. When the alarm finally went off in the pre-dawn darkness, I was up like a shot, dressed and ready before my dad had even finished his coffee.

I'll never forget the feeling of heading out to the farm that first morning. In the blue-black stillness, it seemed like the whole world was holding its breath. As we drove, I caught glimpses of other hunters' headlights winking from driveways and distant fields.

Settling into the deer stand in the gray half-light, I was a thrumming bundle of nerves and excitement. Every rustle in the underbrush made my heart race. Turkeys exploding from the branches nearly toppled me from my perch. As the sun crept over the horizon, every shadow and shape seemed to morph into the form of a deer. I hardly dared to breathe.

I didn't even see a deer my first morning, but that was okay. I had so much fire in my heart that I was ready to sit there forever waiting.

I never got a shot off that season. Afterward, I threw myself into scouting and preparation with a single-minded focus. I spent countless hours walking the field edges, studying tracks and sign until I could read the landscape like a map. I took every chance I got to ask the hunters around town, pumping them for every tip and trick they'd picked up over the years. Slowly, the rhythms and patterns of the woods began to reveal themselves to me.

The true test of my readiness came the following year. After another round of what seemed like endless preparations, I was as ready as I could possibly be. My father and I set out before dawn, driving through our small town as it slowly woke up. The sight of other hunters heading to their own spots was both comforting and exhilarating; I was finally one of them.

We arrived at our hunting spot, a place steeped in personal history—it was the same woods my grandfather had hunted. The deer stand we set up was a product of our own hands, crafted in our shop from square tubing and plywood. Every step in this process felt intensely personal and significant.

That morning, as I sat in the stand, the world around me began to stir. The sounds of nature waking up mingled with the distant hum of corn dryers and the occasional rustle of wildlife—each noise amplifying the anticipation of what might happen. Despite the excitement, my first morning in the stand passed without a single deer sighting. Yet, this did not dampen my spirits; instead, it fueled a deeper desire to continue, to prove myself capable of joining the ranks of the hunters I looked up to.

A few days later, on the last morning of the hunt, I finally saw my chance. A doe appeared, walking gracefully around a small island of trees, perfectly positioned for a shot. My heart raced as I took aim and pulled the trigger. The shot broke the morning silence, and I watched anxiously as the doe ran off.

The moments that followed were tense and filled with second-guessing. Had I hit her? The lack of immediate evidence suggested I had missed. My father, emerging from his own stand, joined me in a thorough search for any sign of a hit. We found nothing. No blood, no trace of impact. It was a miss.

Despite the initial disappointment, this experience did not deter me. If anything, it solidified my resolve and passion for hunting. The anticipation, the preparation, the quiet moments of waiting, and even the missed opportunities—they all contributed to what became a lifelong passion. It was in these woods, gun in hand and heart full of hope, that I truly found my place in the tradition that had captivated me since childhood. I learned out there that I really was a sportsman because all I wanted to do was stay on that stand the rest of the day and continue to hunt. I really wasn't willing to give up. I wanted it so bad. That's when I knew that this was going to be a lifelong passion of mine.

No one could get me to sit still when I was a kid, but all of a sudden, you put a piece of metal up against a tree and you couldn't get me to move. I hated getting up early, but during hunting season, I'm the first one up. Early on, I saw my own raw obsession coming out in those ways. My hunts stayed with me when I went to bed at night, and then I'd dream about being on that deer stand. It was the only place in the world I wanted to be.

Those early seasons, even when I came home empty-handed, were some of the best times of my life. I'd make the rounds to all the neighbors, enjoying that sense of community, just to see what everyone else brought in, to hear them jaw about the one that got away over beers. I lived for the buzz around deer registration time down at the bait store, watching the lucky ones roll up with their harvest to get tagged, joining in on the tall tales and what-ifs.

One of the best things about deer hunting season was the abundance of homemade deer sausage and summer sausage that everyone wanted you to try. After a successful hunt, there were so many nights at home processing the deer and making a variety of dishes from the meat we had harvested. I remember tasting venison for the first time and thinking it was the best thing in the world. Beyond just the hunt itself, the entire process from harvesting the animal to cooking the meat made hunting so cool—quartering it out, packing it out, deboning it, and finally getting to savor that hard-earned food that you couldn't just buy at the grocery store. There were so many laborious steps of love and passion that went into each piece of wild game meat before it graced the table —from locating the animal to dragging it out of the woods to meticulously butchering it—but that made the final meal all the more rewarding.

The hunt I'll remember forever was my second deer season. I was 15 or 16. After missing my shot at a doe the first year, I was on a mission to redeem myself. One freezing sunrise, hunkered in my stand while perching on a 5-gallon bucket, I tried a couple grunts on my call. A buck crashed through the slough behind me. I grunted again, and he came charging right to the field edge. I can still feel the cold butt of the gun against my cheek as bore down on the deer. The shot was true. He dropped on the spot.

I was so keyed up I practically jumped out of the stand. When I reached the buck, I saw I'd have to put in a finishing shot. After, I took off running for my dad, who was waiting in his truck. I could barely get the words out to tell him I'd done it. He followed me back and helped me field dress it. I've never felt an accomplishment like I did in that moment.

Punching my tag, registering my first buck, a seven-pointer, and showing it off to all my friends —those moments crystallized something in me. I'd put in the time and paid my dues. Through patience, persistence and skill, I'd finally joined the ranks of real hunters. It was a bone-deep fulfillment that's kept me pushing myself as a hunter ever since.

Jack's first deer

That's the thing about success—it makes you hungry for more. It makes you want to test your limits and find out what you're really capable of. For me, that meant setting my sights on bow hunting next and mastering an even greater challenge. It meant going deeper into the terrain, toughing it out longer, and dialing in my equipment and technique with precision.

What I've come to understand, reflecting back, is that the discipline of hunting, the relentless pursuit of achievement, is the same fire that forged me as a soldier. Both require strength, endurance, and grit. Both demand a keen eye, a steady hand, and nerves of steel. But above all, both cultivate virtues of the highest order—humility, patience, respect, courage.

It's no coincidence that so many of our military members cut their teeth as hunters and outdoorsmen. The greatest generations of American soldiers were molded by hardship and self-reliance and the character that comes from pitting yourself against nature's tests. There's just no better way I know to build the mental toughness because at the heart of hunting and being a soldier is a creed of never quitting, never shying away from a challenge, and always showing up and giving it your best. It's about constantly pushing past your perceived limits and striving to be the best version of yourself to earn your accomplishments through dedication and sacrifice. And it's about taking pride in doing things the right way, in the knowledge and skills you've honed, in your unwavering commitment to the mission.

These are the values I first absorbed as a young hunter. And these are the values I've carried with me into battle, into my darkest and finest hours as a soldier. Because in both arenas, it's that spirit of relentless pursuit—that drive to face down any obstacle, charge toward any challenge, dig deep, and find a way to triumph—that makes all the difference.

As the years went by and the hunting seasons blurred together, the lessons of the woods began to imprint themselves on my character. Hunting taught me patience above all else—the patience to sit in stillness for hours, waiting for the perfect moment. It taught me resilience in the face of discomfort, whether it was shivering in a frosty stand or trekking for miles through rain and mud. It taught me the importance of meticulous preparation and attention to the smallest details.

But perhaps the most profound lesson was one of connection and belonging. In the hunting community, I found a second family—a band of brothers bound by a shared passion and code of ethics. We celebrated each other's successes and lamented each other's losses. We pushed each other to be better hunters and better humans. In the military, I would find echoes of that same deep camaraderie and sense of shared purpose.

Many of the skills and traits I developed as a young hunter served me well in the Army. The patience and discipline, the comfort with discomfort, the ability to read terrain and conditions—all of these translated seamlessly to the demands of military life. But it was more than just practical skills. Hunting had instilled in me a perspective that saw beyond the individual, a willingness to let go of ego and personal desires for the good of the mission and the team.

Even more fundamentally, hunting shaped my character in ways that would prove crucial in the face of unimaginable adversity. It had taught me to lean into challenges rather than shy away from them, to see obstacles as opportunities for growth and self-discovery. In the long, painful months of recovery after my injury, I would draw on those same reserves of patience and perseverance that I had first tapped as a boy in the deer stand.

Now, as a father myself, I see the hunting tradition through new eyes. When I take my own kids out into the woods, helping them learn to move with patience and purpose, I feel the weight of generations stretching out behind and before us. I understand now that hunting is about so much more than harvesting an animal. It's about finding our place in the great web of life. It's about embracing both the beauty and the brutality of the natural world and learning to make peace with the wilderness within ourselves.

I am grateful for the wild places and wild creatures that shaped me, that continue to shape me.

They have made me who I am—a soldier, an outdoorsman, and a father. As I pass on these traditions to my own children, I do so with a sense of responsibility and hope. The hunt, after all, is never really over. It goes on, season after season, generation after generation, connecting us to the deepest parts of ourselves and to the world.

> *I've known Jack Zimmerman since he was just a kid, full of energy and curiosity. I remember taking him on his first deer hunt, sitting by that log, telling him over and over to keep his head down and sit still. Even then, I saw the determination in him that would later define who he is.*
>
> *I've had the privilege of watching Jack grow into the man he is today, and I've always been proud of him. Jack's resilience and strength are things I've always admired, and I'm honored to have been a part of his journey.*
>
> *— Paul Dauk*

Chapter 3

Adaptability

We were sea duck hunting off the coast of Massachusetts. We flew into Boston and drove down to hunt with a retired 101st Airborne Division veteran called Captain Jack who was a guide out there. I remember we went out the first morning. We got the boat as close to the sand bar as we could. My buddies had to throw me over their shoulders and try to get me onto the shore.

It was very difficult being in the ocean—the sand bar, the waves, the tide, everything working against us. We had a lot of adversity we were facing. My friends didn't want to drop me, and the ground underneath them was a sandbar that was unstable. They were trying to carry me to shore without drowning me. It turned out to be quite the task getting me to shore the first day, with me trying to grab one or two guys and get me up there.

In some ways, it reminded me of duck hunting with my high school buddies in the river bottoms, which had been a whole different kind of thrill from hunting deer. Slogging through in the dark, decoys clanking, breath puffing in the cold air. Setting up in a blind together felt like suiting up for a big game, all of us hyper-attuned, whispering, waiting. When a flock would drift in through the mist and we'd rise up firing in sync—those moments of teamwork and triumph were electric. And now, as an adult, I was having an experience that was parallel to those hunts as a teenager, but it was so different from anything I could have imagined back then.

We sat out there all day, and we were super lucky. The eiders were moving really well that day, and it was just a phenomenal day overall. But now my friends had to get me off the sandbar that day with the same struggle.

We went out that night and were having dinner, talking about how we could adapt to the situation of getting me from the boat onto shore and making it an easier transition. We knew that we could keep doing it the way we were doing it, but it was incredibly difficult. We needed to change up our situation so we could continue to hunt out there and make it a little bit easier and safer for everybody.

As we're sitting there eating, we come up with the idea that we're going to steal the bedsheet off the hotel bed. I'm going to sit in the middle of the bedsheet and four guys can grab onto it instead of two. They all have a handle and they can put the sheet over their shoulder.

The next day, we headed out in the boat after getting me in. We broke ice leaving the harbor in the ocean, which gives you an idea of how cold it was out there in January. We made our way out to the sandbar again. My buddies set me on the sheet, they all threw me over their shoulders, and we pushed out onto the sandbar and set me down.

I moved in and out all day with the tide, and we continued to shoot our ducks. We had a second day of great shooting—the ideal day on the water, despite the challenge of getting there. That day drove home just how crucial adaptability is when overcoming adversity. Overcoming challenges in pursuit of your passions teaches us a lot. We have to understand that the way we always intend to go out and do things might not always work. We have to be willing to be fluid, find that adaptability, and understand that things aren't always going to go the way that we want them to go.

Sea duck hunting

We should expect things in life to be hard, but we also need to expect to overcome them. When I think of adversity or adaptability in the field, we have to expect things that we set out to do and plan to do aren't going to go according to plan, and we have to adapt, simply never quitting.

> *There are moments in your life where you realize that your misfortune has actually made you stronger. Not stronger in the physical sense but mentally, emotionally and spiritually. What makes those misfortunes turn into your own personal strength depends on how open you are to reflect, process and learn.*

What makes that process easier is if you share your struggles with others and seek out like-minded friends to share their struggles with you. There is an old saying that goes, "Learn from other peoples' mistakes so you do not have to repeat them." This, in my opinion, also applies to learning from other peoples' success and perseverance. Just as defeatist attitudes are contagious, so are attitudes of adaptability.

I have considered myself fortunate to have the family that I was born into, but I am also grateful for the friends I have acquired over my life and their contagious traits that they have "infected me with." When I first met Jack, I was standing on a tarmac at a municipal airport watching a private jet get taxied up to a crowd waiving American flags.

Jack Zimmerman

I had heard of Jack from an old schoolmate of mine who turned out to be Jack's Army recruiter. As I watched him get off the plane to be welcomed home by our community, it was hard not to notice his smile. Despite him being a young man whose life had just been irrevocably changed, there it was: a smile.

At that time, I was a late-twenty-year-old husband, father, and Iraq war veteran searching for my next mission. Through mutual veteran connections, I got to know Jack more, and eventually we grew into close friends as only those who served in combat can. As time went on, I began to see the impact Jack had on our friend group and also saw our impact on Jack's life. I'd like to say this happened organically or by luck, and that might be true to some extent when you meet someone by happenstance and have the opportunity to really get to know them.

But I now realize that when you surround yourself with individuals who are the right kind of "contagious," you not only become infected but you grow to also become "contagious." Initially, it is a *choice, but if you do choose it, eventually, it just becomes who you are and who is around you.*

That is the power of Jack's story and his message of adaptability. He may not be in your life, but there is no reason that his philosophy cannot or should not be. Make his message your own and make yourself the kind of "contagious" that is worth spreading because why would you ever want to spread something else?

— Michael McLaughlin

Chapter 4

Making Changes

When I woke up in the hospital, I remember wanting to get back out there more than anything. That was one of the biggest things, just wanting to be in the woods, hunting again. It was one of the biggest drivers I had lying in that hospital bed. But at first I didn't know how I was going to do it.

My first support system was the guys who were wounded before me. Understanding that they had gone through similar challenges and were back out in the woods already, living good lives, gave me hope. If they could do it, I could do it.

It really taught me not only how to adapt to get back to something I wanted to do, but it also helped me realize that I had to adapt to everything else around me in this world—the world wasn't going to adapt to me.

If I could find the drive, the energy, the patience, and all the virtues it takes to push through those adversities of getting out and doing something I really wanted to do, I could craft those same types of skills to get through everyday life too. There were the things that I didn't have as much drive for, but now I had the patience for them because I had proven myself through something I really loved.

Missing legs, missing most of my arms, being confined in a wheelchair, essentially, I wondered how I was going to get out in the woods and go to the places that I wanted to go. It took a lot of people in the hunting world to help me hunt the things that I wanted to hunt going forward. I hunted with a lot of wounded warriors and guys who had been wounded in similar situations, and I learned from those guys in a mentorship capacity.

As I began adapting to my new way of moving in the world, I was creating a new baseline of ideas of what hunting was. So as I grew and started hunting different things down in Texas—hogs, doves, and exotic game like rams and black bucks—I had to rely on my mentors and the people that had been hunting these things before.

What I learned was that when I lean on the people who have been there, who are more than excited to teach and help us understand how to hunt this game, relying on a mentor can expedite where we want to be in the woods skill-wise a lot faster. It kind of took me back to my military training, relying on the guys who have been there before, the guys that have been to war. A trend was starting to become apparent. I could see the threads that I was just beginning to realize were woven through my life: the importance of mentorship and the power of leaning on others.

When you find yourself going into places over in Afghanistan, you have to rely on the people that have been there before, the guys that can teach you the techniques, that know where to go and what to do and how to stay alive in those situations. I fell back to those skills now in the woods and relied on the guides that have been hunting in these areas forever. I leaned on them to help me get into the right places.

There were a lot of times when, if I wanted to get to a hunting blind, there might not be a clear-cut path to get my wheelchair to the spot I wanted to get to. Or the door on the hunting blind might not be big enough. I'd have to figure out ways to get into position in those hunting situations, like jumping out of my wheelchair and moving into another chair.

Sometimes I'd go out in public and wouldn't know where the curb cut was in the beginning. Or I wouldn't know how to get into a building because it wasn't accessible, but I really wanted to be there. A lot of people would just turn around and leave in those situations, but I was able to have the patience to work through the obstacles and not panic. I could see that there is always a way—I just have to adjust how I'm going to do it.

One of the first skills I had to adapt was bow hunting. With my changed body, if I needed to cock a crossbow, I'd have to figure out how to hook up the cocking mechanism, figure out how I was going to crank it and hold it with my other arm that wasn't as strong, or lean up against something. I had to do whatever I needed to get that thing cocked back. It was the same as trying to figure out how to get a jar open in the kitchen. It was those same skills that I had to learn—the patience, the understanding of how to use my new body according to what I had, and figuring out how to overcome those problems.

As a young, confident kid who wants to go out

and be the best, you see some of the top hunters in the country shooting archery. You have to get so close to the animal to harvest it with a bow. The effort it takes to become good with a bow, you have to shoot a lot to be successful with one.

That's what my friends and I did when I was a teenager. Any time we had free time, we weren't shooting baskets, we were shooting our bows. That's what we really enjoyed doing. I found a lot of passion in practicing, getting better, and pushing myself to become a better archer.

The first time I ever went out turkey hunting with a bow, my friend Andy and I snuck out that morning because we didn't have school, we had a rehearsal that day to go practice walking for graduation.

We went out and I harvested a turkey. I remember throwing it into my dad's shop and then, since we lived right next to the school, we ran to graduation practice. Then coming home after, cleaning that turkey. It's just one of those memories, even though I knew I had to be somewhere that morning, something so important as walking for your high school graduation practice, I still thought it was more important to go try to shoot a turkey.

Lying there in that hospital bed, the idea of ever hunting again seemed like an impossible dream. The woods and fields that had always been my refuge now loomed as insurmountable obstacles. How could I possibly navigate the rugged terrain, the icy streams, the dense brush and steep ridges that were challenging enough when I had all my limbs? The prospect was daunting, to say the least.

But something deep inside me refused to let go of that dream. Hunting wasn't just a hobby for me —it was a part of my identity, a connection to something primal and essential. Out there in the wilderness, I felt alive and whole in a way I never did anywhere else. I couldn't imagine giving that up, no matter how much my physical circumstances had changed.

As soon as I was able, I started figuring out how to adapt. I went hunting with other wounded warriors who had faced the same challenges, learning from their experience and ingenuity. I relied on the knowledge and support of my fellow hunters in a whole new way. Slowly but surely, I began to rebuild my skills and my confidence.

I still haven't successfully shot a compound bow again. I had to switch over to a crossbow. I was very fortunate that, after I was hurt, companies stepped up and helped make a crossbow for me at the time, before they really even became that popular, a crossbow that I could cock back with a reel using what I had left of my arms.

It got me back out in the woods and gave me the ability to hunt again with a bow. That's where I first started to learn that I could still do the things in this world that I wanted to do, that I had so much passion for. I had to accept that—that I was still out there doing what I love to do, just doing it a little differently. And that was okay.

There's something about being in the outdoors and giving yourself a goal, trying to accomplish something that day, and that didn't change after I was wounded. You have to use your brain capacity to put yourself in the best position possible to fulfill your mission. But a lot of it is being alone in that stand, alone with your thoughts.

We live in a very loud world. Even when you're in bed at night, there's so much noise around you. It may not even be a noise that's in your face, but it's that your phone is lying next to you, or that you should probably email that person back. All the other things that are going on in your world. But when you go hunting, all of a sudden you're in a place where you have no service, and maybe there's no one else around. No distractions.

At first, when I started getting back out there hunting, I found my thoughts going to a lot of dark places, but it was good for me. In life, you have to deal with the bad before you can move forward. You have to take out the thing that's bothering you the most first before it hits you in the face.

As a soldier, I'd had hard experiences long before my injury. When you're deployed, you don't have time to grieve. There's no time to be sad. It's a time to get mad—to get even. That's how we looked at it then. You never have time to process exactly what you went through. You never realize how horrendous life around you really is, in a sense. There's a lot of death. There's a lot of violence. Your whole day is based on violence and death—or preventing violence and death.

I was pulled out of that experience and had to process everything that had gone on for the nine months that I was there, every event that happened, every gunfight, every loss, every time a friend got wounded or killed...There was just so much to unpack. But being out there in the woods, it gives you that space and stillness to finally confront it all.

When I was going through all those things, I also had to figure out how to become a better communicator. Because I had to be able to communicate my problems, my daily worries and frustrations, all those things I had in the beginning of trying to figure out what the best new version of myself was going to look like.

I had to be able to communicate better with people and learn how to not only express my feelings but communicate the things I saw around me that were becoming problems. I learned how to communicate with my doctors and tell them what hurt and what needed to be fixed. I had to be able to communicate to people that I was worried about what daily life was going to look like when I got out of the hospital, so those people could communicate back to me that I wasn't the first person going through this and hundreds of people before me had learned how to live independently. I used those lessons to face my adversities.

Something about using the people who came before me to face adversity

I went through occupational therapy, the one thing I ended up hating the most in all my rehab, but it was a necessary evil that I had to accomplish. Being able to communicate not only my worries, the things that I didn't know how I was going to work through in life, the things that I was going through, being able to communicate with other guys that had been wounded in my situation and being able to learn from them and take advice.

At that point in my life, I learned to listen more instead of talk more because I was learning so much about life, and everything was so new to me. I really had to focus in on how to communicate with people to try to make my life as easy as possible.

> *As very close childhood friends, Jack and I spent a number of our teenage years hunting together and learning from each other.*
>
> *As Jack mentions, our first archery turkey hunt—I remember this vividly—we were young and eager. I remember sitting in the ground blind with both of us drawn back on two separate turkeys that seemed to sneak up on us so quickly. Nerves set in as we quietly counted to three so we could both shoot at the same time.*
>
> *After the release, we quickly realized*

there was only one turkey flopping around as the others scattered. Jack had hit his, and I had missed mine. Although I was bummed that I had missed, it was so fun watching Jack fly out of the blind like a little kid to chase down his turkey and hold it up with pride. This is a hunt I will never forget.

I also have memories duck and goose hunting with Jack in these same years. Trucking through muck and cattails to find birds wasn't always easy, but at our age, we seemed to like to do things the hard way. Although not every hunt was successful, it didn't matter if we killed one bird or a limit; we still had so much fun.

It's no surprise Jack still has and always will have the passion to hunt and pass on these skills to his kids.

— Andy Krenik

Chapter 5

Unbreakable

One of the most pivotal moments in my journey back to hunting was a mountain lion hunt in eastern Montana a few years after my injury. It all started when I met a guy named Dan while deer hunting in Buffalo County, Wisconsin. Dan told me his favorite thing to hunt was mountain lions. When I asked if he thought it could ever be a reality for me to harvest a mountain lion, he said, "Absolutely."

The idea was born during those deer hunts in Wisconsin at my buddy Kyle Bushman's place. Kyle and I dreamed up the possibility of making me the first double amputee to hunt a mountain lion. Kyle was instrumental in turning this dream into reality. He and Dan traded a mountain lion hunt, and Kyle suggested taking me along.

Dan reached out to others in the houndsman community who were familiar with eastern Montana, where the mountains weren't as extreme. He found some guys out there who wanted to help take us out. Kyle, who I had been deer hunting with in Wisconsin, stepped up in a big way. He picked me up and drove me all the way out to Montana.

Dan drove across the state from Western Montana to meet the rest of us in a small town in southeastern Montana. We were just a bunch of people who came together to try to do something that had never been done before—to get a double amputee up a mountain, find a mountain lion, and harvest that cat.

We were different people bringing different skill sets and different roles to the mission, but we all knew that we were going to put the same amount of effort into trying to have a great outcome. Without Kyle's initiative and Dan's connections, this incredible adventure could never have happened.

The first day of hunting, we pulled in to our destination and a man named Buckshot told me, "The guys are back there. I believe they found a good track. Why don't you head back there and see if you can find the guys and we'll try to get you on a mountain lion."

I remember throwing all my gear on as fast as I could because I thought I was going to be going up the mountain almost immediately. It turned out that hunting mountain lions required a great deal of patience, though. As soon as I got there with my license, they cut the hounds loose. We hung out for a while, and it took about an hour and a half for the hounds to finally put that cat up a tree.

Some guys made their way up there and got to the cat while we were trying to find a way for me to get up there, and they started getting excited about what they'd found—a great cat for me to harvest. They got a fire going and got the hounds around the tree, and my guys threw me in a sled and started pulling me up the mountain. I just kept digging in the snow as hard as I could while they hauled me.

Every time we stopped, I could hear the dogs a little bit louder. While the howling of the dogs grew closer and closer, we kept digging until we finally got up to the top of the divide where the cat was with the dogs underneath the tree.

Eventually, I was sitting on a 40-foot ledge with the tree in front of me, about 40 yards away. I was almost at eye level with the cat, and I was looking at this tree swaying in the wind, but I couldn't spot it. I remember thinking, "How is there a 130-pound cat in this tree, and I can't find it?" I finally did, though, and began situating myself, propping my gun on a makeshift rest using someone's hiking sticks. But the hiking sticks just weren't cutting it as a rest.

My friend Brandon, who lost his leg overseas, took his prosthetic leg off for me to use as a rest for my rifle. I lowered my cheek to the stock, breathed out, and squeezed the trigger. The shot rang out. For a sickening moment, I thought I had missed. Then the cat burst from the branches like a coiled spring unloosed, bounding up the far drainage.

My heart sank. I had hit him, but not well enough. Now we had a wounded lion on our hands, and it was on me. I cursed myself for not making a better shot.

The dogs were after him in a flash as we piled me back into the sled and followed, trudging through the snow. When we caught up to them again, the animal was back in a tree, visibly injured now. I raised my rifle, steadied, and fired—and finally accomplished what we set out to do. I had harvested my first mountain lion.

I wanted to whoop, but it caught in my throat.

Sitting there amidst the mountains, the hounds baying behind me, and my brothers gathered around, I was suffused with a bone-deep sense of humility and gratitude.

These men—some who started out as strangers and were all now my brothers—had carried me up this mountain, step by strenuous step. It was their expertise, their perseverance, and their faith in me that had made this moment possible. I had squeezed the trigger, but this was a team effort in the truest sense.

There in the thin, whipping air of that Montana ridgetop, I felt whole and capable. I understood, perhaps for the first time, that the essence of who I was had nothing to do with the limbs I was missing. With the right people at my back and the right mindset, I could still reach the highest pinnacles, both literal and metaphorical.

That lesson would be reinforced again and again in the hunts to come—particularly during a black-bear hunt in the northern Minnesota wilderness, just shy of the Canadian border. A friend had gifted me his tag, a special honor for wounded veterans. Another had offered his bear camp, a snug outpost amidst the towering pines and shimmering lakes of Northern Minnesota.

But getting to the bait sites proved trickier than we had anticipated. Heavy rains had turned the trails to soup, a formidable challenge for my track chair, a powered wheelchair rigged up like a miniature tank to plow through brush and rough terrain and shallow water. What I had envisioned as a quick jaunt stretched into a slogging odyssey through sucking mud and water.

When I finally reached the bait site and tucked myself into the blind, I was already anxious and nervous that I had made too much noise getting out there. As the time ticked by, day after day with no sign of a bear, those doubts began to gnaw at me. Maybe I was fooling myself, thinking I could outwit a creature as canny and sensitive as a black bear. Maybe all the scent and noise of my ungainly approach had long since driven them into the next county. Maybe I just wasn't cut out for this anymore.

I had almost convinced myself that harvesting a bear wasn't realistic when I raised my head and the unmistakable outline of a bear at the bait site proved me wrong. My self-pity evaporated in a surge of adrenaline.

I raised my rifle to my cheek, found the crease behind his shoulder, lined up my bead, and breathed out. The shot was true. He bounded off a few steps into the trees, and I heard him crash. It was over almost before I could process what had happened.

Sitting there in the blind, anxiously waiting to go find my bear, I felt a rush of emotions as complex as the forest around me. Elation, of course—the hunter's high of a successful harvest. But more than that, a profound sense of humility and respect.

This creature had tested me in ways I had not expected, forced me to confront my own shortcomings and self-doubt. He had not submitted easily. Securing this harvest had demanded every scrap of patience, skill, and perseverance I possessed, and then some. In the end, I realized, that struggle was the real gift.

It's a truth I've learned again and again in the

years since my injury—that it's through adversity that we find out what we're really made of and make our biggest personal gains. Every setback, every obstacle, is an opportunity to dig deeper, to adapt and overcome. And often it's the people around us, our community, that give us the strength and belief to do so.

This was never more apparent than on that mountain in Montana, where a group of relative strangers came together to help me achieve what many would have considered impossible. In the military, we learn to rely on our battle buddies without question or hesitation. As a hunter, I've found that same spirit of solidarity and shared purpose.

There is something about the pursuit of a difficult game that forges unbreakable bonds between people. Maybe it's the long cold hours in a blind together, or the adrenaline of the stalk, or the shared joy of success and disappointment of failure. Or maybe it's just the understanding that out there in the outdoors, we are all ultimately on the same team, all equally humbled before nature.

I know I could not have become the hunter I am today—could not have reclaimed that integral part of myself—without the wisdom and generosity of so many others.

From the old hands who shared their hard-won knowledge, to the friends who lent tags and hauled gear and pulled sleds, to the fellow wounded warriors who showed me the way forward—I owe a debt of gratitude that can never be fully repaid.

The attempt to pay it forward, to be that person for someone else, is the best expression of that gratitude. In the end, hunting isn't really about the trophies on the wall or the meat in the freezer. It's about the connections we make, with the land, with the game we pursue, and with each other. It's about being part of something larger than ourselves, a timeless cycle of challenge and growth and wonder.

Losing my legs made me worry, at times, that I had lost that forever. Instead, I found a deeper understanding of what the hunting life really means. It's not about physical perfection or prowess. It's about heart and spirit and the unbreakable bonds between fellow sportsmen on the journey. It's about digging deep and pushing through and coming out the other side stronger than before.

> *I have known Jack several years, although he is the kind of person you feel you've known a lifetime. Jack inspires me to be a better person, not to dwell on shortcomings but celebrate your gifts and your blessings.*
>
> *Jack's love of God, family, country, and living life to the fullest is incredible. Being counted as his friend is a true blessing. I do not know anyone else with as much courage, love, and devotion to live to the fullest while inspiring all he meets. I cherish Jack's love, friendship, and energy—ain't nothin' holding him back! Jack may no longer be 6-foot-3, but in my eyes, he will forever cast a 10-foot shadow. He's a hell of a man!*
>
> *— John Streiff*

I met Jack over 10 years ago, shortly after he responded to a social media inquiry for a Whitetail hunt for disabled Veterans that I was sponsoring in Western Wisconsin. It became pretty obvious after talking with him that we had a lot in common. We both grew up in the Midwest in small farming communities. We followed a lot of the same sports teams. We both enjoyed hunting, fishing and our time in the outdoors. We both enlisted in the Army around the same age and graduated basic and AIT as 11BRAVOs from Fort Benning, Georgia. We both shared the GWOT rite of passage and, within a couple of years of each other, were deployed to different ends of Southeast Asia.

Whether we were scheming up ways to hunt White-tailed Deer, Ducks, Geese, Pheasants, or Mountain Lions, I always enjoyed spending time with Jack. Regardless of his physical impairments, he was up for anything; he never complained about his circumstances, never portrayed himself as a "victim," and had a sense of humor that was infectious to be around!

There's a definitive reason for every

person that God puts in our lives...I really never knew how important it was to have a role model like Jack until I was faced with my own set of unfortunate circumstances when I was diagnosed with Terminal Kidney Cancer in the Spring of 2022. I've gotten through a lot of incredibly difficult and dark days by internalizing how Jack was able to fight through his own battles and come out smiling on the other end...and for those lessons, I'm truly grateful.

— SFC Kyle Bushman

Chapter 6

Man's Best Friend

When it comes to hunting, there's nothing quite like having a good dog by your side. Over the years, I've had the privilege of sharing the field with some incredible hunting dogs, each one leaving an indelible mark on my life and my hunting experiences.

One of my earliest hunting partners was a chocolate lab named Max. Max was our family pet, but she'd never hunted before the first time I took her out after pheasants. I knew that if I let her off leash, she'd run so far ahead of me that I'd never have a chance to get a shot off. So I came up with the idea of tying her to my waist with a long rope.

Looking back, it probably wasn't the smartest plan, trying to handle a shotgun with an untrained dog tied to me. But I was determined to make it work. We set out into the fields and ditches, Max pulling at the end of the rope as I stumbled along behind her.

We walked for hours, zigzagging through the tall grass and brush. I was just about ready to call it a day when I noticed a change in Max's behavior. She started getting birdy—her tail was wagging faster and faster, and her nose was working overtime, sniffing the air with intense focus. As she got closer and closer, I could feel the energy thrumming through the rope that connected us.

As we approached the end of a narrow strip of cover, the grass began to thin out. Max was practically vibrating with anticipation, and then, in a heart-stopping burst of wings and feathers, a big rooster pheasant exploded out of the grass mere feet in front of us, cackling the whole way.

It all happened so fast that I didn't even have time to get a shot off. The bird was up and gone in a blink. But in that moment, I wasn't disappointed. On the contrary, I was thrilled for Max. She had just achieved her first real flush. Overcome with pride, I dropped to the ground right there and lavished her with praise and affection.

That's the beauty of hunting with dogs. It's not just about the birds you bring home. It's about the journey you take together, the bond you forge through shared experiences and triumphs. Watching Max work that field, seeing her natural instincts kick in, that was the real reward.

Years later, after I returned from Afghanistan, I found myself yearning for a hunting companion again. I was living near a lake with wetlands in my backyard, and I would often go out to shoot a few ducks. But without a dog to retrieve them, I always had to call a buddy to come pick them up for me. Plus, I missed waking up and training every morning like I had in the military, and working with a dog would give me that daily purpose. I knew it was time to get a new hunting companion.

Enter Moose, a black Labrador retriever that came into my life not long after. I had big dreams for Moose and I was determined to train him to be the best hunting dog he could be. I reached out to a renowned dog trainer named Chris Smith, who had been out of the game for a while due to a successful battle against throat cancer, which made it difficult for him to train dogs.

Chris agreed to help me train Moose, and we started working together every single day. Little did I know at the time just how pivotal Moose would become, not just in my development as a hunter, but in my overall recovery and well-being.

At that point, I was still very much in the thick of dealing with the aftermath of my injuries. The phantom pains were excruciating, and the memories of what I had experienced in Afghanistan were still raw and vivid in my mind. Whenever I felt myself slipping into those dark places, I would grab Moose and we'd go out to run a blind or a mark or work on new skills. It kept my mind occupied and gave me a reason to keep pushing forward.

Moose became a lifeline. When the phantom pains got really bad, he would jump up onto my lap and lie there, the warmth and weight of his body against my residual limbs providing a relief that no medication could match. Our daily training sessions gave me a sense of purpose, a mission to focus on beyond my own struggles. I missed *wanting* to get up and train every day and get better at something. It was really hard for me to do at that point—but he was always excited to train together, and that helped get me off my butt.

Over time, Moose and I honed our skills as a team. With Chris's guidance and a lot of hard work, we made history by becoming the first handler-dog pair to earn an AKC Senior Hunter title with the handler operating from a wheelchair. It was a proud moment, but more than that, it was a testament to the unbreakable bond that had developed between us.

Jack with Chris Smith (right) and Moose

Today, Moose is still by my side, a constant companion in the field and at home. That's the power of a good dog. They're so much more than just a tool for the hunt. They become an extension of yourself. Their drive, resilience, and unconditional love remind you, in moments of doubt or darkness, of the unbreakable bonds that tie us to the natural world and to each other. I had gone from being a little kid sitting on a hill watching Chris run his dogs on his ponds to training alongside him, and I could not be more grateful to him for making my dog-handling dreams come true.

Jack and I stayed in contact while he was overseas. He had expressed interest in becoming a dog trainer. The day came when I heard of his injuries, and the whole community came together with worry about how this was going to play out. Jack was in Texas now in recovery. I spoke briefly with his mom and dad to check how he was doing. It was going to take time for his recovery.

I have trained many dogs and handlers to perform in competitions. Also, I've taught them to become good dog trainers. So, I bought a pup and trained him myself with the intention of giving him to Jack when he got home. His recovery was very long. Not knowing when this would happen, I sold the dog. When Jack did come home, he was looking for a pup. That's when he found Moose.

I told him to bring him out in the mornings, and we would train together. We worked every day for two years. Jack asked me to run Moose in a hunt test to get his title. I said, "You run your own dog. I'll come along and help." That's what we did. There were a few times Moose made mistakes and didn't pass the test. Jack asked, "Now, what do we do?" So, we went home and trained harder till the next trial. Jack ran his own dog from his track chair through the Junior and Senior AKC titles. It was an amazing thing to watch and be a small part of!

Some years before this, I had completed treatment for tongue cancer and had a full neck dissection with all my teeth removed due to radiation. When he was asked by a reporter, "What do you call your kennel?" Jack replied, "No Teeth, No Legs, No Problem."

There is nothing he cannot do. I'm very proud to have been a small part of a great team, Jack and Moose.

— Chris Smith

Chapter 7

Leaning on Others

As a young soldier, I prided myself on my toughness and self-reliance. Needing help was not something I was comfortable with—it felt like an admission of weakness, a chink in the armor of my carefully cultivated image. But all that changed in an instant on the battlefield in Afghanistan.

Lying there in the dirt, all four of my limbs essentially blown off, I realized with startling clarity that I could no longer do everything on my own. If I wanted to survive, if I wanted any kind of future, I would have to learn to accept assistance from others. It was a profound shift in perspective, one that didn't come easily to me. But as I lay there, my life hanging in the balance, I had no choice but to surrender to the care of my fellow soldiers and the medic who fought so hard to save me. I had to learn how to give everything over and accept all the help that I could get and understand that sometimes in life it is okay to ask for help.

My lesson in accepting help from others came early—while I was still lying on the battlefield, bleeding out. In that moment, I vowed never to turn away anyone who wanted to help me, no matter how easy or difficult the task. Accepting help changed my life completely, not only in terms of receiving assistance but also in trying to offer help to others whenever I can. When I woke up in the hospital, I couldn't do anything for myself. I had to rely on the help of others and trust that they would do their best to save my life. As time went on and I started to venture back out into the woods, I needed people to help me get there. However, I also wanted to gain my own independence with each step I took. I didn't want everyone to do everything for me; I just needed enough help to get me where I wanted to be until I could do things for myself again, to the extent that I was able.

That lesson carried over into my long recovery. Waking up in the hospital, I found myself completely dependent on others for even the most basic tasks. With no limbs to speak of and my remaining stumps heavily bandaged, I couldn't feed myself, dress myself, or even scratch an itch. It was a humbling and often frustrating experience for someone used to being so fiercely independent.

But as time went on, I began to see the value in allowing others to help me. Each small act of assistance, whether it was a nurse adjusting my pillows or a fellow amputee showing me a new trick for getting dressed, was a step forward on my journey of healing. Slowly but surely, I started to regain some measure of autonomy, learning to do for myself whenever possible. But I also learned the importance of asking for help when I needed it and accepting that help with grace and gratitude.

This was especially true when it came to getting back outdoors and reclaiming my identity as a hunter, as I had with the black bear and the mountain lion. I knew I couldn't do it alone—the physical challenges were too significant. If I wanted to return to the woods and fields that had always been my sanctuary, I would need the support and expertise of others.

At first, it was my fellow wounded warriors who showed me the ropes. These were men who understood intimately the struggles I was facing because they had faced them too. They taught me how to navigate rough terrain in a wheelchair, how to shoot with adaptive equipment, and how to read the land and the game with new eyes. Their camaraderie and shared sense of mission was a powerful force that helped me push through some of the darkest days.

As I ventured further into the world of adaptive hunting, I found myself relying on the kindness and know-how of all sorts of folks. There were the old-timers who took me under their wing, sharing a lifetime's worth of hard-won wisdom. I met guides and outfitters who went above and beyond to accommodate my needs and help get me back out there.

Each of these individuals played a crucial role in my journey of rediscovery. Without their generosity and belief in me, I don't know if I would have found my way back to the outdoors and the sense of purpose it provides. Their willingness to help, to share their knowledge and their passion, was a profound gift—one I can never fully repay, but one I strive to pay forward every chance I get.

Even to this day, there are still many situations where I need help. It's not realistic for me to think that I can harvest a deer and drag it out of the woods by myself. I'm incredibly grateful to have so many people willing to help me and take me out hunting. This brings me to one of the legacies I want to leave behind: inspiring others to help people get back outdoors. Whether it's taking your grandfather out on the boat one more time or accompanying your uncle on a pheasant hunt, it's important to appreciate and give back to those who helped you experience the outdoors by dedicating a day to take them hunting. It's so rewarding to return the favor—to get them out there the way they did for me.

Now, when I meet young hunters, especially those who are facing their own challenges, I try to impart the lessons I've learned about the power of accepting help. I know how hard it can be, especially for young men, to admit when they need assistance or guidance. There's so much pressure to be self-sufficient and go it alone, but I've seen firsthand how transformative it can be to let others in, to be vulnerable and open to the wisdom and generosity of your community.

I tell them about the incredible experiences I've had thanks to the people who were willing to help me, whether it was the buddies who hauled me out into the slough for that unforgettable duck hunt, or the mentors who taught me the finer points of spotting and stalking a deer. I try to show through my own example that accepting help isn't a weakness—it's a strength, a way of deepening your connections to others and to the natural world that sustains us all.

I remind these kids that this isn't a one-way street. There is so much reward in reaching out and accepting help, and there's just as much reward in offering it. Some of my most meaningful experiences in the outdoors have come from being able to share my own hard-won knowledge with others, or simply making it possible for someone to get back out there and do what they love, even if it's just for one more hunt.

There's something incredibly powerful about being part of that chain of generosity, of paying forward the gifts that have been given to you. From helping an old-timer climb back into the deer stand one last time to mentoring a young person through their first turkey season, the act of enabling someone else's joy and success is profoundly fulfilling.

In the end, that's what the hunting life is all about—not just the pursuits and triumphs of the individual, but the shared experiences and bonds that tie us all together. It's about being part of something bigger than yourself, a community of people who understand the primal pull of the wild and the deep satisfaction of providing for yourself and others. By being open to giving and receiving assistance, we strengthen the fabric of that community and ensure that the traditions and wisdom of the hunt will be passed down to future generations.

For me, learning to accept help taught me the true meaning of humility, gratitude, and interconnectedness. It showed me that even in our darkest and most difficult moments, there is always hope to be found in the kindness and generosity of others. In the end, we're all in this together—all part of the same grand and timeless pursuit, all dependent on the land and on each other for our survival and our joy. By embracing that interdependence, by being willing to give and receive the gift of help, we ensure that the hunting life will endure, in all its richness and complexity, for generations to come.

> *I remember meeting Jack Zimmerman shortly after he arrived at BAMC. He was confident and resolute that he would face the challenges of rehabilitation head-on. I was very impressed by his approach to handling the situation and their overall*

maturity in dealing with a situation that most young people never even have to think about. He had an infectious energy and was diligent about his rehab. He inspired other young soldiers coming into the CFI to do their very best in their own rehabilitation. I am grateful to know Jack, and I am thankful for his friendship.

— Will Lyles

Chapter 8

Camaraderie

One of the biggest gifts the hunting life has given me is the camaraderie—the bonds forged through shared challenges and triumphs in the field. This is especially true in the veteran community, where the love of the outdoors often goes hand-in-hand with the desire to serve and the deep understanding of what it means to be part of a team.

Since my injury, I've had the privilege of hunting with some true legends like Larry Weishuhn, the wildlife biologist and author whose TV show earned him the nickname "Mr. Whitetail," and Jim Zumbo, the famous writer for Outdoor Life. I remember reading Zumbo's articles as a kid, soaking up his tips on fishing and cooking wild game. Hunting with him was a surreal experience. He had this way of finding humor in any situation, like the time he plucked a head of broccoli right out of a field while we were hunting moose in Maine and started munching on it. (Really—who brings ranch dressing into the field?)

As much as I've enjoyed rubbing elbows with the big names, it's the hunts with my fellow wounded warriors that have meant the most. There's just something about being in the woods with guys who understand on a bone-deep level what you've been through, who know without saying a word the demons you're wrestling with and the healing you're chasing.

When you're out there together, sitting in a boat or huddled in a blind, the rest of the world and all its noise just falls away. You're focused intensely on the task at hand, but at the same time, your mind is free to wander and process. I've had some of my most cathartic moments in those quiet spaces, finally able to confront the survivor's guilt and grapple with the whys and what-ifs of my injuries.

But I've also found immense healing in the simple camaraderie, the easy laughter and smack-talking and the deep conversations around the campfire at day's end. Sharing stories, swapping jokes, reliving the highlights and lowlights of the hunt—it's a comfort like no other.

There's a particular brand of dark humor and brutal honesty among vets, especially those of us who have seen combat. We'll rag on each other mercilessly, but we'll also open up about our struggles in a way we might not with others. There's an unspoken understanding that we're all fighting our own battles, but that out here, we have each other's backs, no matter what.

One of my favorite memories is of a duck hunt in North Dakota a couple of years ago. I was invited out by a veteran nonprofit that puts together adventures for wounded vets. I hadn't hunted ducks on open water from the cattails, like I had as a kid, since my injury, and I had all but given up on the idea. Logistically, it just seemed impossible with my limitations.

But these guys were determined to make it happen. They scouted out the perfect spot, a cornfield slough thick with cattails, and figured out a way to get me out there. I remember the afternoon of the hunt, when clouds hung low over the plains of North Dakota. My buddies loaded me into a little jon boat. I had no idea how it was all going to work, but I could feel the anticipation thrumming between us all.

They pulled me slowly through the slough until we reached the edge of cattails where the ducks were sure to pass. The guys lifted me out of the boat onto a dog platform in the water, got me settled with my shotgun, then hunkered down on either side, our shoulders brushing companionably.

And then we just waited, sitting back with Cohiba cigars from Havana and awaiting the evening flight.

When the ducks finally started moving, fast and furious in the cloudy evening, it was magical. We moved as one, rising to shoot, whooping with the thrill of it. I felt more alive, more vital and connected and truly part of something, than I had in ages.

Back out on the water with my buddies again, I was suffused with gratitude—for the duck and for the men who had made this possible through sheer force of will and loyalty.

Duck hunting in North Dakota

That's the power of shared experience. It gets you outside of your own head and reminds you that you're part of a larger community and a grander story. The outdoors has a way of leveling the playing field, stripping away all the labels and expectations until what's left is the elemental you, the pure and timeless rhythms of the natural world and the simple joy of good company.

I've found that same spirit in camps all over the world. No matter where I go or what the quarry, the campfire circle is the great equalizer. Political differences and personal troubles fall to the wayside. What matters is the stories, the laughter, and the ritual retelling of a day's adventures.

Those experiences take me back to nights in Afghanistan, huddled with my battle buddies on the porch outside our tent, trading snacks and tall tales, leaning on each other's strength to ward off the fear and loneliness. The terrain and the stakes might have been different, but the camaraderie was the same—that sense of being knit together by something bigger than yourself, of relying on the guy next to you to help shoulder the load.

That's something I didn't fully appreciate before my injury—just how much I drew from the people around me, how much their belief and support got me through even the toughest moments. When I was lying there in the dirt in Afghanistan, my life bleeding out, it was the faces of my brothers-in-arms that I clung to, their love and loyalty that gave me the will to keep fighting.

And it was the same after, through the surgeries and the rehab and the long, hard slog of rebuilding some semblance of a life. Every card and care package, every visit from a buddy, every opportunity to get back out there in the field with men who understood—it reminded me again and again that I wasn't alone, and I still had a place and a purpose.

When I'm sitting around the campfire now, swapping stories and draining another Diet Coke, I'm acutely aware of what a gift it is, how lucky I am to have these men in my life. We've seen each other at our best and worst, and we're still showing up, still finding ways to have each other's backs.

There's a quote I love from a guy named David Coggins—he said, "The outdoors doesn't fix you, but it tests you, and there is no better mirror than a good friend." I think that cuts right to the heart of it. Hunting isn't some magic cure-all. It's hard and humbling and it forces you to confront your own shortcomings. But when you do it with people you trust, people who know your demons because they have their own, it becomes something more.

> *Jack Zimmerman is a testament to what a motivated mind and a spirit to succeed can accomplish.*
>
> *When guests come to our duck camp, we want to show them a first-class waterfowl experience by providing great camaraderie, good food, and superb duck hunting action. When we found out Jack was coming to our veteran hunt, we were stoked because he's a fellow Minnesotan.*
>
> *However, we also had some apprehension, as while we had hunted with guys in chairs, we'd never hosted a triple amputee. We hunt from ground blinds and marsh*

stools, and Jack demonstrated his motivation and success mindset right away.

First, he was willing to try. His spirit was strong.

Second, Jack also explained to us that success wasn't in the results and that no matter what the result, the process of effort and trying was the win. And his infectious smile as we talked through this added even more fuel to our fire.

On our opening hunt in a cut bean field, we used ratchet straps on his "legs" to hold him in the ground blind. The first duck of that hunt, and many more ducks, belonged to Jack.

Later in the week, Jack balanced on a dog platform in 3 feet of water—and the ducks cooperated—and Jack was on fire, dropping ducks left and right. We ended up with four days of hunting, three limits, and two very important reminders—motivation and spirit are undefeated.

Throughout the week, Jack was engaging, fun, honest, uplifting, and the guy you want to spend more time with.

Everyone has challenges; Jack reinforced that it's what we do to overcome those challenges that determines our character. Cheers to Jack for being an ambassador for all of us—and being a helluva good shot to boot!

> *— Ted Carlson, curator of Greenheads in Your Face; Somewhere, North Dakota*

Chapter 9

Wetting a Line

For me, fishing is a pursuit that puts a laser focus on the special bond that forms among sportsmen. Out on the water, it's a different vibe than hunting, where you're often sitting solo in a deer blind or creeping silently through the woods. In the boat, conversation flows as naturally as the current. There's just something about that rhythm of casting and retrieving, the shared anticipation with every bite and run, that loosens the tongue and opens the heart.

I've always enjoyed fishing, but after I was wounded it took on a new significance. In those early days of recovery, when I was wrestling with pain and uncertainty, sneaking away to wet a line became my therapy. Whether I was chasing catfish on the Tennessee River or crappie in my backyard, the familiar rituals grounded me and gave me a sense of peace and purpose when my world had been turned upside down.

Catfishing in Alabama

There's just something magical about a day on the water. It starts with the anticipation as you launch the boat, the early morning sun glinting off the surface and the whole day stretched out before you, ripe with possibility. Then there's the sensory feast as you motor out—the wind in your face, the slap of the waves, the reflection of clouds and trees dancing on the ripples. Already, you can feel the stress of daily life slipping away, replaced by deep contentment.

The excitement really builds when I'm rigging

up and getting those first lines in the water. Every cast is a fresh start, a new opportunity for that heart-stopping tug on the line. I can't help but dream of state records and once-in-a-lifetime fish. Even if it's a spot I've fished a hundred times, there's always that voice in the back of my head saying, "This could be the day." That never gets old, which may be the thing that drives me.

As much as I relish the thrill of the bite and the bend in the rod, though, it's the time between catches that I've really come to cherish. Some of my best memories are of easy conversation unspooling between friends as we work a shoreline or drift across a flat. On the water, the pressures and posturing of daily life fall away. Discussions range from the profound to the profoundly silly, and revelations rise to the surface that might never be spoken on dry land. I've laughed myself breathless and I've teared up at confidences, all to the soundtrack of water lapping at the hull.

A special bond happens in a boat, a camaraderie and communion that I haven't found anywhere else. When your buddy boats a big one, their victory is yours too. And when you lose a fish at the last second, as we all do from time to time, your partner is there to commiserate and encourage, already plotting the next cast and the next chance.

When I was lying there on the battlefield, I saw snippets of my greatest hits—big bucks and turkeys, limit days, and celebratory photos. But what lanced through me, what I wanted more than one more breath, was the faces around those moments: my buddies laughing around the poker table at deer camp, the fellow soldiers who had become closer than brothers. It wasn't the achievements that mattered most in the end. It was the people I shared them with.

That's what I try to re-create every time I head for the hills now, banged-up and scarred and missing a few parts, but hungry as ever for that feeling. Hungry for the hilarity and humility of good friends, for the spark of understanding and acceptance that needs no words. For the singular satisfaction of working together against long odds, and the soul-deep rightness of breaking bread after, telling the old stories and writing new ones in the embers.

It's a legacy I want to pass down to my own kids—not just the skills of outdoorsmanship but the value of standing by your people through thick and thin. Of showing up to do the heavy lifting, literally and figuratively. Of being the kind of friend and hunting partner you'd want in your own worst moment. And of appreciating the hell out of that friendship in all the moments between.

That's the real reward—the thing that no taxidermist can mount but that you carry with you forever. It's knowledge that whatever comes, you've got a place around the fire, a shoulder to lean on, a brother to raise a toast and rest your burdens with. That's the true north of the hunting life, and it shines brighter the more it's shared.

> *When I think of Jack Zimmerman, the first word that comes to mind is resilience. We met 10 years ago while pheasant hunting, and I knew right away that Jack was someone special.*
>
> *After that hunt, I invited Jack to go catfishing. At the time, I wasn't quite sure how I was going to get him in the boat that first time, but we figured it out.*
>
> *Now, I joke that I don't know how to get him out of the boat because he loves it so much.*
>
> *That first trip was more than just a fun day on the water; it was the beginning of something much bigger.*
>
> *Our shared love of the outdoors and*

the connection we forged on those early trips led me to start Patriot Catfishing, a nonprofit dedicated to getting disabled veterans out on the water.

But we do more than just fish. We hunt together, share stories, and enjoy the camaraderie that comes from spending time in the great outdoors.

Over the past decade, Jack has become not just a friend; he has become family.

I never met anyone with more drive, spirit, and a positive outlook on life than Jack. His never-quit attitude is second to none.

As a combat-wounded veteran, Jack has faced challenges that most of us can't even imagine. Yet, he has never let those challenges define him. Instead, he has used his experiences to fuel his passion for helping others, whether it's through his writing, his motivational speaking, or his support of Patriot Catfishing.

Jack's ability to turn personal pain into a source of strength for others is truly remarkable.

Beyond his resilience, what stands out about Jack is his authenticity. He's the kind of person who stays true to his values, no matter what.

Whether he's sharing stories from the battlefield, talking about his love for the outdoors, or working on his next big project, Jack is always real, always genuine, and always committed to making a positive impact on the world around him.

Jack's dedication to his country, friends, and community is unparalleled.

He's the guy you can always count on, whether you need advice, a helping hand, or just someone to listen. His loyalty and integrity are qualities that I admire deeply, and they're a big part of why I'm proud to call him my brother.

— Kevin Breedlove

Chapter 10

The Next Generation

The day I took my son pheasant hunting for the first time could have been a flashback from my own childhood. We were out in southern Minnesota on a friend's property, joined by a few of my veteran buddies and our bird dogs. As we gathered our gear that crisp autumn morning, I went over the safety talk with my son—keeping the barrel pointed in a safe direction, finger off the trigger, identifying his target, and being aware of what lies beyond.

These were the same fundamentals drilled into me as a kid, the building blocks of responsible hunting. But that day, it was my turn to pass the wisdom along, to be the mentor. I felt an immense sense of pride and responsibility as he walked between me and one of my buddies, all eyes and ears.

We flushed our first rooster and he watched, wide-eyed, as it exploded from the grass in a whirlwind of feathers, my shotgun barking. His excitement was palpable, a fever I recognized instantly—it was the hunting bug taking hold. Over the course of that long cold day tramping the fields, I watched the tradition kindle in my son, saw him pushed to his limits and rise to meet each new challenge with grit and bravery. A hunt forces a reckoning, stripping away the veneer to reveal one's core mettle. Out there trudging through the brush, shivering on stand, the child comes face-to-face with adversity in its rawest form—the elemental struggle encoded in our spiritual DNA. It's humbling and transformative on a cellular level, a reminder of our deep tie to the natural world.

I marveled at the growth happening before my eyes on that hunt and marveled at the man my son was becoming day by day. With each flush and shot and retrieval, I sensed him standing taller, resolve fortifying. By the time we headed back to the trucks that afternoon, he had taken his first strides into a tradition spanning eons—a journey of self-discovery and life's grand cycles honored and accepted.

It filled me with immeasurable gratitude to be the one lighting that path for him. Not just passing down the skills of wing-shooting and dog-handling but instilling the core values that the hunting life imparts—patience, humility, perseverance, reverence for our quarry and the land that sustains us all. These are the seeds from which ethical, honorable hunters are born.

Jack's first hunt with son William (third from left)

There's something vitally important about teaching our youth where their food comes from, what it truly costs when we take life to sustain our own. I want my son to understand the gravity of that transaction, the responsibility we accept as hunters to be prudent stewards of the natural resources in our care. It's not about the killing, but the circle of life. It's a lesson in our place in that cycle, a reminder of our duties to the future.

That's why conservation and land management are such critical parts of the mentor's role. We can spark all the passion in the world for these young people, kindle an insatiable fire to hunt and be immersed in the outdoors. But if we don't also instill in them the drive to preserve and restore wild lands and waters, to fiercely protect the habitats that sustain their passion, what kind of legacy are we leaving?

I'm proud to pass this ethos down to my kids, along with the stories and lore of our country's hunting heritage. I want them to look at the deer mount over the fireplace or the dusty decoy in the basement and feel that sense of continuity, of being part of an unbroken human tradition stretching back to the dawn of our species. The highs and lows, the triumphs and heartbreaks, the sacred rituals and hard-won wisdom—it's their birthright, assuming they honor it with the same tenacity as their forebears.

My younger son, Benjamin, has gravitated in a different direction from William—Benny's the fish whisperer in the family. While pheasants and deer hold zero appeal for him, you can dangle a lure or bait anywhere within a hundred-mile radius and he's liable to materialize on the spot, eyes gleaming with excitement.

I'm just as delighted to be passing the tradition to him.

Son Benny with fresh catch

We may have been born in different eras, but the feeling of setting the hook and leaning back into a fish is eternal, a shared coded experience transcending generations. When he lands that catch of a lifetime, he'll be tapping into the same primal well of satisfaction as some Neanderthal forefather along the ancient Nile, firelight glinting off his obsidian spear.

It's easy to take that freedom for granted when

you grow up surrounded by open spaces and game lands, which is why I feel so strongly about introducing young people to the doctrine of public land stewardship as early as possible.

That's the greatest gift I can hope to impart to my own sons and their generation—not just the traditional skills of rod and rifle, but the awakening to a life of conservation and advocacy for our wild places. It starts with patience and humility on the hunt, with learning to exist gracefully and gratefully within the rhythms of nature. Then it builds toward a sense of duty to uphold the delicate biological balances that make such wildness possible, a duty that must be renewed and re-consecrated with each generation. Severing that thread would be a tragedy.

One day in Afghanistan, I had to go sit up in a guard tower. I was thinking about those kids and how unfair it was that they had gotten caught up in something that had nothing to do with them. They'd stepped on an IED after we had gone through a village chasing the Taliban. After the Taliban left and we left, the IED did not get disarmed. Those kids were out playing soccer when they stepped on it. Two of the three died, and the third was severely injured.

Up in that guard tower, I told myself I had to

do something when I get home to make sure these kids have some kind of legacy—that something good came out of this situation. My way of finding good in this was me being able to go out and try to create a legacy for these kids who never had a chance to do it for themselves.

Not sure where to start, I started teaching firearm safety to kids. It was my first way of giving back and helping a generation of Americans understand how lucky they are. Kids here have opportunities just because they were born where they were. They have the immense luxury of taking freedom for granted, and I wanted to help them appreciate it through something I loved— the passion for the outdoors.

After I was done being a kid's age, I hadn't spent much time around adolescents. I was a student, then I joined the Army as an infantryman. When I was growing up, nobody ever asked me if it was a good idea to get out of my hometown area for a little bit and see the rest of the world. It was all about getting the best job with good benefits and a pension, staying on that career path, playing it safe, and taking one vacation per year. That was going to be my life.

I knew deep down that was not who I was, though. That was not the life I wanted to live, but I felt like everybody around me only gave me one option. The only way out that I saw was to join the Army. I thought I could get away for a bit, get paid, go do something great for my country that I always wanted to do, and contribute to the war effort in a meaningful way instead of being a bystander. The Army would check all these boxes.

As much as I value my time in service, looking back, I wish an adult had told me directly that it's okay to take risks and blaze your own trail for a while. Experiencing the world beyond your hometown opens your mind. When I got back from Afghanistan, I wanted to find a way to help guide kids to understand they have all these opportunities available to them that they should take advantage of.

I never got pushed to temporarily postpone the straight-and-narrow life trajectory and explore other options as a young man. In hindsight, I absolutely should have taken a few years to get outside my small worldview and gain other experiences first. The Army ended up being my gateway, which I'm thankful for. But I didn't have to make that extreme move.

After I came home, spending time with these kids meant so much to me. I shared my stories and experiences with them, and I helped them handle firearms safely so they could go out and enjoy the outdoors as much as I do. I knew what the outdoors could do for them because of everything it had already done for me up to that point.

That work led me to start a trap shooting team for the high school here with kids beginning a new phase of their lives and looking forward to the next. I tried to be the person who believed in them, like people who believed in me. There were so many things taught on the trap field—respect, handling firearms properly, cleaning up and helping out. We created a culture that was amazing to be a part of.

My goal was to give those kids the idea that they could do anything they wanted in this world, that the only thing stopping them was themselves. I helped them grow not just as shooters but as people. I showed them that these outdoor skills translate over to anything in life they want to get better at. They just have to put time and effort into it every single day. I asked the tough questions about their motivations and dreams that adults didn't pose to me at that age. I prompted them to consider all possibilities before making life choices by default.

That's what I tried to pass on to my students—the understanding that they aren't locked into any pre-determined future. If they dream big and put in the effort, any path is possible. Our only limits are the ones we impose on ourselves.

Some kids that age don't have enough positive influences showing they can be anything they want in life. I tried to be that voice telling them the only thing holding them back is themselves. Watching them gain confidence in their marksmanship abilities, but also internalizing bigger life lessons about dedication and perseverance—that's what was most rewarding.

Safety is always a top priority when taking kids outdoors. We didn't go to extremes—we covered the basics like filing a hunt plan, checking gear and vehicles, and making sure everyone was prepared for the conditions we'd encounter. The main thing was giving kids the best possible experience out there. When I was a kid, if you complained about being cold or miserable on a hunt, that was seen as unacceptable—you just toughed it out.

I wanted to create positive memories that would make them passionate, lifelong sportsmen. There's no point grinding through an awful experience you'll end up resenting. If a kid was cold or wet, we'd head back to the truck until conditions improved. I'd rather spend extra for a guide to put us on the fish than have an epic fail that turns them off the sport forever. Memorable successes are what ignite that fire to keep exploring the outdoors.

With high schoolers, there was less opportunity for intensive wilderness survival training. My focus was more on helping them develop a healthy outdoors mindset—and steering them to ask the right questions about their goals and priorities. When I'm working with kids, whether it's through hunting or shooting sports or just talking about life, I try to give them the same kind of straight talk and unconditional support that my own mentors gave me. I want them to know that they're capable of more than they realize, that there's a whole community of people ready to lift them up and cheer them on.

It's also about stewardship. When I was young, instilling conservation principles from the start wasn't as urgent—we simply had more untouched wilderness areas to roam and explorable nature surrounding us.

Today's reality is starkly different, and it's only been a few decades. That's why I see sparking passion for hunting and angling as planting half of the seed. The other equally vital half is nurturing the philosophy of giving back as future stewards of the lands that made their passion possible. It's a responsibility I didn't fully grasp at their age, with how much surrounding wilderness I took for granted.

Today, not only has more land been altered for farming and cities and suburbs, but some hunters have created adversities through unsportsmanlike things out in the field. While there is more public land available now, with limited private land access combined with the same number or more hunters, public lands get hunted increasingly hard. This adds pressure not just on the animals in their habitat from more hunters present, but also crowding amongst hunters themselves. Consequently, hunters are traveling farther to more remote areas seeking the experiences they desire away from crowding.

The scope of what kids need to learn is certainly more comprehensive today. They're learning not just skills like shooting, hiking, and hunting ethics, but overarching philosophies like seeing themselves as active conservationists from day one. If new generations don't commit to protecting America's rapidly diminishing outdoors from an early age, I'm pessimistic about what wilderness traditions will still exist for their grandkids. It's my goal to prevent that.

Since my injury, I've gained a new perspective on what really matters in life. When you come that close to death, it clarifies your priorities pretty quickly. You start to realize that so many of the things we worry about and get worked up over just aren't that important in the grand scheme of things. What matters is the experiences you've had, the people you've connected with, the sense that you lived with purpose.

One of the ways I've tried to find that purpose is by giving back and helping others discover the healing power of the outdoors. I've been really fortunate to have some incredible mentors who helped me get back to doing what I love, even when I wasn't sure it was possible. Guys like Kyle, who drove all night to get me to a mountain lion hunt in Montana, and Brandon, a fellow leg amputee and wounded warrior who helped me steady my rifle on that same hunt. Having people like that in my corner, people who understood what I was going through and were there to support me no matter what—that made all the difference.

So now, I try to be that person for others. Whenever I can, I look for opportunities to share what I've learned and help people find their own path to healing and growth in the outdoors. If I don't go out there and share my stories, my sacrifices are a waste. If nobody can learn from the things that I went through, then I'd be wasting an opportunity to help the people that are coming behind me. I've always said that to battle through adversity, we have to look to the people who came before us and fought through things that were much harder than we ever had to fight through.

What I can tell you is there's no one right way to be an outdoorsman. You don't have to do things the way everyone else does them. Whether you're chasing whitetails with a compound bow or fishing a stocked pay pond, what matters is that you're out there, participating in nature and challenging yourself to grow. It's not a competition or a measuring stick—it's a personal journey, and everyone's path looks a little different.

> *I felt excited and happy to finally be out hunting with the guys. From the moment we pulled up to the field until we left, I had a huge smile on my face. When the first bird flew up, I'll never forget watching the barrel on Dad's gun following the bird across the sky.*
>
> *He had a perfect shot, and I just remember seeing feathers flying every-*

where. I loved offering to carry the birds every time we got one down. At the end of the hunt, I got to try the pheasant, and I couldn't believe how juicy and delicious it was.

— William Zimmerman, age 11

Hunting isn't really my thing. I don't like having to be so quiet and sit so still. When you're fishing, you can visit with people, and you're constantly casting your line in and out. I love being out on the water, away from everything else, away from all my chores... My whole mind is just on fishing.

The first time I pulled a fish up and was holding it for a picture, I just kept staring at it and thinking, I couldn't believe I really did it, I really caught a fish. Getting that first one just made me so excited for all the fish I was going to catch that day.

— Benny Zimmerman, age 9

Chapter 11

Gratitude, Awe, and Resilience

When I think of awe, I think of elk.

After being wounded, I was invited up to Sheridan, Wyoming to hunt elk. We arrived at the ranch late in the evening, spending the night in the lodge with the other guys. I remember waking up the next morning and rolling out onto the deck with my Diet Coke. As I sat there in the stillness, I heard my first elk bugle echoing through the Bighorn Mountains. The sound stopped me in my tracks, and my soda plummeted to the floor.

I had heard recordings before, but to experience that primal scream in person—it filled me with an almost electric anticipation. Harvesting an elk had always been a dream of mine, the pinnacle of big game hunting in North America. Now, with that haunting bugle, the obsession grew even stronger.

We spent the day scouting, glassing different herds and looking for the right bull. Driving those rugged mountain roads, swapping stories with my guide and soaking in the majesty of the Bighorn Mountains, I felt a deep contentment. This was where I belonged, despite everything that had happened. The wounds, the surgeries, the grueling therapy—none of it could take this from me.

When we finally located the herd and the bull we wanted, the real work began. We worked to get ahead of them, my guide helping my maneuver into position. As we got into position, I could feel my heart pounding against my ribs. The elk moved through the plain above us, grazing slowly. The bull I had my eye on was one of the last to step out into the grassy expanse. I settled the crosshairs and squeezed the trigger.

At the shot, the herd exploded into motion. The bull kicked and started to run with them. I chambered another round and found him again in the scope, leading him slightly. The second shot anchored him. I couldn't contain the shout that burst out of me. I turned to my guide and we embraced, both grinning like fools, babbling our thanks and congratulations.

But the real moment of awe came when I finally put my hands on that bull. Running my fingers over the rough curve of his antlers, tracing the lines of power in his still-warm flank, I was overwhelmed with gratitude and reverence. I had dreamed of this moment, visualized it countless times. Now here I was, in this expanse of sky and stone, blessed to participate in the hunt.

Looking around at the faces of my companions, all of us streaked with sweat and dust and blood, I realized that this was about so much more than taking an animal. It was about rising to meet a challenge, about reconnecting with something elemental in myself. It was about finding my place in the world again, even if that place looked different now.

In that moment, with my heart still pounding from the thrill of the hunt, I knew that I would never stop seeking these experiences. No matter what obstacles I had to overcome, I would find a way to return to the wild places that restored my soul. And I would do everything in my power to share that gift with others.

That's really the crux of it. Hunting, for me, isn't about the killing. It's about the totality of the experience—the preparation, the effort, the camaraderie, the deep engagement with the natural world. It's about pushing yourself to the limit and coming out the other side with a clearer understanding of who you are and what really matters.

I think that's why I'm so passionate about getting others outdoors, especially those who have faced hardships or feel disconnected. I know firsthand the healing power of a mountain sunrise, the confidence that comes from provide for yourself, the soul-deep satisfaction of hard work rewarded. These are the things that can help us find our way home, no matter how lost we feel.

That's the key, really. Whenever we face adversity in life, we have a choice. We can try to go it alone, muscling through on stubborn grit. Or we can look to our community, to those who have walked the path we're on and come out the other side. In the hunting world, that kind of mentorship is sacred. There's always someone willing to take a new shooter under their wing, to share hard-won wisdom and hot spots alike.

For me, that generosity has been a lifeline. It's allowed me to reclaim not just the activities I love, but the identity that goes with them. When I'm out there chasing bugles or whistling wings, I'm not a damaged veteran in a wheelchair. I'm a hunter, an equal participant in the age-old dance. And that matters more than I can say.

I'll keep seeking out those moments of awe and those encounters with wildness that remind me of my place in the great scheme. I'll keep pushing myself to the edges of what I thought possible, and then past them. And I'll keep sharing those adventures with anyone who will listen, in the hopes that they too might find their own reservoir of strength and wonder.

I truly believe that a life outdoors—a life spent engaging deeply with the rhythms of nature and our own primal heritage—is a life well lived. It's a life of humility and gratitude, of challenge and growth. It's a life that demands the best of us and returns the favor a hundredfold.

That's the legacy I want to leave: a way of being in the world that honors the interconnectedness of all things, and our responsibility.

The bull on that Wyoming mountaintop was a gift I'll never forget. No matter how broken I felt, the hunter in me endured. As long as there were still wild places and wild things, I had a reason to keep pushing, to keep reaching for those moments of grace and awe.

That's a truth I carry with me now, whether I'm propped in a deer blind or navigating the obstacles of daily life. The hunt is always on, in one form or another. And as long as I'm breathing, I'll be out there chasing it, marveling at the beauty and mystery of a world that never fails to surprise me.

Having gratitude for this life is something that keeps me grounded. It makes me self-aware and thankful for the things that people around me are doing to help. Without gratitude, I cannot appreciate anything in life. If I cannot find things to be grateful for or show gratitude toward, then I am not looking in the right places or doing the right things.

When life strips so much away from you, the appreciation you have for things is what becomes most important. We learn how fast things that we were once grateful for can be gone. I know that the memories I am making are what I will take with me when I leave this world.

A big part of those moments worth remembering is the people involved, knowing that I would be able to take those experiences with me. I find the most gratitude in the people who surrounded me, willing to put themselves through something difficult to help me accomplish my goal. It was an incredibly selfless act on their part to help me fulfill a dream, even after I had something stripped away from me that I thought would make it impossible to ever achieve that dream someday in my life.

It may seem obvious that the defining adversity of my life was being severely wounded in Afghanistan. Losing both legs and suffering grave damage to my arm, I was confronted with obstacles that could have broken my spirit. In those first harrowing moments on the battlefield, clinging to life, a pivotal choice emerged—would I surrender to darkness and bitterness, or make sure I lived a life worth watching?

The words of the surgeon on the tarmac that day gave me that essential spark of hope to fight for. "If you can just stay awake five more minutes, I promise you your life." In that vow, I found something to cling to, a reason to persevere through the agony. Holding that promise in my mind's eye, I mustered every fiber of determination to meet the surgeon's challenge.

That singular moment became emblematic of how I have chosen to face down adversity ever since—by zeroing in on the potential for perseverance and growth, rather than surrendering. When the anguish of phantom limb pain threatened to overwhelm me in those first years of recovery, I would look for the people and pursuits that could reignite my sense of purpose.

For a long time, that driving purpose was simply getting back into the woods and rediscovering my passion for hunting. The prospect of feeling the cool autumn breeze on my face again, of matching wits against formidable quarry, propelled me through the grueling rehab regimens. I also drew immense strength from the community of fellow injured veterans who understood the unique struggle of redefining oneself after catastrophic trauma.

We did not go it alone but leaned on each other for the grit and creative solutions to overcome. Whether fashioning adaptive equipment or hauling one another's gear over rough terrain, we embodied the creed of "no one left behind." Our shared hardships became a bonding forge, from which we emerged stronger and more determined than ever.

As I slowly regained my capability in the outdoors, I came to recognize the tremendous value in choosing gratitude over resentment. Yes, parts of my former life were gone forever. But I could be endlessly thankful for the parts that remained—my passion, my family's love, my brothers-in-arms who stood by me. Most of all, I was grateful for the new lens of appreciation that adversity had gifted me.

Where I once took the grandeur of nature for granted, I now beheld it with a profound sense of reverence and humility. Every flush of a pheasant, every glimpse of a bull elk through the pines, filled me with a childlike awe that I worried might have become dulled without my injuries. I found myself newly attuned to the sacred cycles of the hunt, the delicate balances of predator and prey. In losing a part of my physical humanness, I had regained a prized connection to something wild in myself.

This deepened gratitude extended to the communities, both civil and military, that buoyed me through the darkest times. As I shared the joys of the outdoors with fellow wounded warriors and passed on traditions to the next generation, I understood my second chance was something to cherish and pay forward.

By choosing to embrace gratitude and seeking purpose, I transformed struggle into strength. Losing my limbs and independence enabled me to fully embrace my interdependence with this world. In doing so, I found truer self-reliance and appreciation for life's grandeur.

The hunt, the voyage of self-discovery through challenge, is never truly over. It continues season after season, generation after generation, connecting us to the deepest wellsprings of our humanity. My role is to pay forward the hard-won wisdom and opportunities I've been given, so that the hunting lifestyle may endure as a conduit to humility, ethical stewardship, and soul-nourishing gratitude.

Teaching kids about firearms safety, conservation principles, and ethical hunting awakened in me a new sense of purpose—to instill respectful stewardship of our natural resources. If I could pass along the same awakening gratitude I experienced, the same humbling appreciation for our place in the world's grand ecosystems, perhaps these youth could help stem the tide of environmental degradation.

In this way, the adversity that nearly took my life has instead become the driving force propelling me into a life of deeper meaning. The hardships endured have allowed me to shed distractions and fixate on what really matters—personal growth, nurturing communities, protecting wild lands and waters for future generations.

By making the conscious choice to embrace gratitude and seek out purpose, I have transformed struggle into strength.

I now have the honor of guiding others over the obstacles that once seemed impassable. Of course, adversity remains an inherent part of the journey, but with a heart brimming with purposeful gratitude, I know I have the perseverance and community to move forward.

> *Jack, after knowing you all your life, working with you on projects, like starting trap team and teaching firearm safety, I would like to congratulate your accomplishments and your ability to accomplish more every day. Teaching and informing people about things that normally get overlooked in today's busy world is a very necessary thing. Good luck on the challenges you are educating people on, now and in the future.*
>
> — *Dave Voss*

Chapter 12

A New Perspective

When people ask me what my favorite or most significant memory is since I started living my post-injury life, I struggle to choose one. I don't rank or compare moments like that anymore. I've learned to see each day as a gift and an opportunity to apply the lessons of yesterday to the challenges of tomorrow.

One of the most profound realizations I had in the aftermath of nearly losing my life was just how much our perspectives shape our realities. Every morning, the first thing I have to do is drag myself from the bed into my wheelchair. It's an immediate confrontation with a tangible reminder of all the trauma and loss I've experienced. And I have a choice in how I let that reality impact my mindset.

I could easily sink into self-pity, lamenting all the hardships I've faced and using them as an excuse to give up, to resign myself to a diminished existence. There are certainly days when that temptation is strong. But whenever I find myself starting to slip into that negative headspace, I think back to the guys who risked everything to save my life by dragging me off the battlefield that day.

Those men—my brothers—knew the dangers they were up against. They understood with painful clarity that every step could be their last, that the IEDs hidden beneath the dirt didn't discriminate. But when they saw me go down, none of that mattered. They didn't hesitate to rush forward to my aid, exposing themselves to incredible risk because one of their own needed help.

In that moment, I had no choice but to place my complete trust in the hands of others. I was utterly helpless—unable to stanch my own bleeding, to splint my own fractures, to do anything at all to ensure my own survival. All I could do was have faith that my teammates would do everything in their power to get me out of there alive, even at the cost of their own safety.

That level of trust, of surrender, was not something that came easily to me. As a soldier, self-reliance and individual capability are drilled into you from day one. But lying there in the dirt, fading in and out of consciousness, I had no choice but to let go. To believe that these men valued my life enough to treat it as their own, to fight for it with everything they had.

And then again, on the tarmac, when the surgeon looked me in the eye and told me that if I could just hold on for five more minutes, he'd promise me my life. In that moment, I once again had to make the choice to believe—not just in his skill, but in his sincerity. I had to trust that he saw me as more than just another broken body to put back together, that my life held inherent value and meaning to him.

Those experiences taught me that sometimes, the greatest act of strength is allowing ourselves to be vulnerable. To place our faith in the goodness and capability of others. I realized that the only way we can fully believe in someone else is when they tell us with complete conviction that they've got us, that everything will be alright—and then back those words up with action. Trust, I learned, is a reciprocal relationship. My brothers on the battlefield, the surgeon on the operating table—

their belief in me helped me find the strength to believe in myself.

When you come that close to death, it has a way of violently shaking all your priorities into place. The trivial and superficial fall away, and you're left with the cold, hard clarity of what actually matters. For me, it all came down to the people in my life. The strength of my relationships, the depth of my positive impact on the world and those around me. The experiences and memories I'd built and the ones I still hoped to create.

Facing down my own mortality forced me to ask myself the hard questions. Had I been a good friend, a good teammate, a good man? Had I lived with intention and purpose? Did the people I cared about know how much they meant to me? Had I used my time and talents in service of something greater than myself? In the end, very little else held any real significance. It was the human connections, the sincere attempt to leave the world a bit better than I found it, that made a life feel well-lived.

So now, even on the days when the physical and mental challenges feel overwhelming, I make the conscious choice to view my circumstances through the lens of gratitude. I am grateful for the men who put everything on the line so that I might have a second chance at life. I am grateful for the medical professionals who poured their skill and compassion into rebuilding my broken body. And I am grateful for the clarity of knowing, without a doubt, what I want to focus my time and energy on going forward.

I won't pretend this shift in perspective has been easy, or that I don't still struggle sometimes with frustration and grief over what I've lost. There are moments when the unfairness of it all wells up like a tsunami, threatening to pull me under. But I've learned to ride out those emotional storms, anchored by the deep knowledge that I am here for a reason. That my life, and what I choose to do with it, matters.

That wisdom is something I wouldn't trade for anything because with it has come a sense of purpose and determination far greater than any physical capability. I understand now, on a profound level, that we are all living on borrowed time. That each new day is an opportunity to show up for the people and causes we hold most dear, to pour our love and our light into the world with reckless abandon.

So when I wake up each morning and make the physically challenging transition from bed to chair, I do my best to also make the mental shift from lamenting my limitations to counting my blessings. I refuse to let the inevitable challenges rob me of precious time and energy that could be spent in service of my larger mission. I choose, again and again, to believe that I am exactly where I'm meant to be, doing exactly what I'm called to do.

That perspective is a gift born of unimaginable trauma. It's a fundamental rewiring of mind and spirit that could only be carved out of devastation. And I'm grateful for the growth and clarity it has brought me because with it comes the knowledge that I can handle anything life has in store. I don't need to wait for someone else to give me permission to believe in myself or to trust my own resilience and capacity for positive impact.

The most meaningful legacies are built not on grand gestures or impressive resumes or even prize-winning kills but on small daily choices. We choose to show up with an open mind and heart. We choose to lend our strength and knowledge to others in their moments of vulnerability. We choose to meet fear and adversity with courage and determination. Those are the choices I now strive to make, even—*especially*—when they push me further than I ever imagined I could go.

It is an honor to have such a great American hero ask me to play a small part in his amazing story. I first met Jack when one of my brothers introduced us about 10 years ago. He told me there is a guy I needed to meet that had been severely wounded in Afghanistan.

I am an avid hunter and shooter, and Paul thought we would get along great together. Well, that was a huge understatement! Jack and I hit it off right away, and we have been shooting, hunting and fishing together ever since.

It is not often you find a new friend half your age that influences your life as much as Jack has influenced mine. His determination to overcome all that has happened to him is truly inspirational.

I have had the pleasure of introducing Jack to many of my oldest and dearest friends in the last 10 years. Many of these meetings have been based around shooting or hunting. To the very last one he has met, they all say about the same thing: "What an amazing attitude that guy has, and his determination is contagious."

As I read his second book, I learned

new things about the struggles that Jack has faced since that tragic day in Afghanistan. But he seldom lets you know that those dark spaces exist; instead he shows you how to overcome what may appear to be insurmountable.

I have met a lot of people in my life, and few have shown courage and toughness like Jack. I have never known Jack to say he could not do something; rather, he will say, "I need to figure out how to do that differently."

I am proud and lucky to call him my friend. It makes me smile whenever we are walking (or rolling) away from each other or hanging up the phone; he will always say, "Thanks, Mark, I appreciate ya."

— Mark FitzSimmons

Chapter 13

Looking Toward the Future

Mine is a life that was fought for many times over. It's a life that others deemed valuable enough to risk everything for. The only way I know to honor that profound gift is by living it as fully and faithfully as I can, one hard-earned day at a time.

As I get older and my priorities continue to shift, I find myself thinking more and more about the kind of legacy I want to leave. I've been blessed to achieve some big goals in the eyes of a sportsman—taking mature animals in far-flung places and being a pioneer of adaptive outdoors. But at the end of the day, what I really hope to be remembered for is being a force for good in the lives of others. I want to use my platform and my experiences to inspire people to get outside, to connect with the natural world and with each other. I want to fight for the things that make those experiences possible—conservation of wild places, responsible gun ownership, access for all. Most of all, I want to leave this world a little better than I found it and help others do the same.

So that's what I'm working toward now. Continuing to push myself as a hunter and an outdoorsman, but also using what I've learned to make a difference where I can. That means showing up for the people in my life, being there to listen and support and guide however I'm able. It means giving my time and my energy to causes that matter, even when it's not easy or convenient. And it means taking every opportunity to share the message of hope and resilience that the outdoors have given me.

I know I still have a lot to learn and a lot of room to grow. But I also know that I'm not in this alone. I'm part of a community of people who lift each other up, who fight for what matters, who never stop striving to be the best versions of ourselves. Together, we can face down any challenge and come out stronger on the other side. That's the power of the unbreakable spirit, and it's a power we all hold within us. My job now is to help as many people as possible unlock it, in whatever way I can. That's the mission, and I'm grateful beyond words to be able to pursue it.

As I look to the future, I see great potential for growth, both personally and for the outdoor community as a whole. We face significant challenges—habitat loss, increasing urbanization, and younger generations disconnecting from nature. But I've learned that challenges often present opportunities, and I believe we outdoorsmen and women are in a unique position to make a real difference.

One of my main goals is to continue breaking down barriers to entry in the outdoor world. Whether it's physical disabilities, financial constraints, or simply lack of exposure, too many people are missing out on nature's transformative power. I want to work with organizations and individuals to create more adaptive equipment, improve access to hunting and fishing areas, and develop mentorship programs to welcome newcomers.

We also need to become more vocal and active advocates for conservation. As those who spend the most time in wild places, we have a responsibility to be their stewards and protectors. This means not just supporting conservation efforts financially, but also getting involved in policy decisions, educating others about habitat preservation, and leading by example in our own practices.

To my fellow outdoorsmen and women, I have a challenge: Let's each bring at least one new person into our world every year. Take a kid on their first fishing trip, help a disabled veteran rediscover their love of hunting, or invite a friend just to get outside into nature. We have the power to ignite that spark in others. Share your knowledge and passion, be patient and encouraging, and remember that every expert was once a beginner.

For those just starting to feel the pull of the wild, don't be intimidated. The outdoor community is full of people eager to help, teach, and share in the joy of discovery. Start small if you need to—a local nature walk (or roll), a day trip to a nearby lake, or even just observing wildlife in your own backyard. No matter what your challenges are—physical, time-related, financial, or anything else that's keeping you indoors—the important thing is to take that first step.

As for me, I'm excited to keep pushing my own boundaries. I can't wait to find out what adaptive technologies will open up more outdoor opportunities for people with disabilities so others can find healing and purpose in nature like I have.

And I'm always looking for new ways to give back to the community that has given me so much.

The future of our outdoor heritage depends on all of us. It hinges on our willingness to adapt, innovate, and welcome new perspectives. It depends on our commitment to preserving the wild places and creatures that make our pursuits possible. And it relies on our ability to pass on not just the skills of hunting and fishing but the ethics, respect, companionship, and deep connection to nature that define true outdoorsmanship.

The path forward isn't always clear, and it certainly isn't always easy. But if there's one thing I've learned, it's that the most rewarding journeys are often the most difficult. So grab your gear, gather your friends, and step out into the wild. The adventure of a lifetime is waiting, and it's up to us to make the most of it.

Remember, every time we set foot (or wheels) in the outdoors, we're not just pursuing game or fish—we're carrying on a legacy, we're writing our own story, and we're shaping the future of conservation. Let's make it a story worth telling, a legacy worth preserving, and a future worth fighting for.

When your life flashes before your eyes, will it be worth watching?

Jack Zimmerman

❝ Anyone who knows Jack and his story knows that he is one of those rare individuals who never looks for an excuse or assigns blame to anyone other than the person staring back at him in the mirror. Because of his amazing outlook on life, he lives in a manner that most outdoorsmen would envy.

After reading Jack's words or listening to him speak, I am always reminded of how much our perspectives matter in life. Often, our perspective can be the single greatest variable in how our day-to-day lives unfold.

Too many people are looking for an excuse so they don't have to take responsibility for their lives not going the way they had hoped. Jack was thrown the ultimate curveball—from being an American soldier one minute to lying in a crater, hanging on to life the next—yet he has never let external circumstances dictate how he wants to live his life.

The pursuit of passion is a driving force in this book. Unfortunately, most people are walking through life without anything that lights a fire inside of them, without anything that requires them to become a better version of themselves, and without anything that calls them to serve a higher purpose.

If there is one stark reminder I took from this book, it is to chase down happiness with laser focus and urgency. Only after finding your inner happiness can you be a guiding light for those who follow.

Life can change in an instant, so make sure there are plenty of good stories to tell about you when you're gone.

Love ya, bye...watch for deer.

— *Andy Shaver*